Course Notes

THE ENGLISH
LEGAL SYSTEM

Catherine Easton

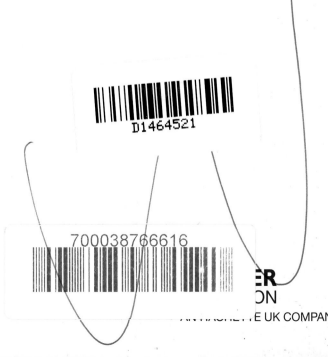

ER
ON
AN HACHETTE UK COMPANY

Orders: please contact Bookpoint Ltd, 130 Milton Park, Abingdon, Oxon OX14 4SB.
Telephone: (44) 01235 827720. Fax: (44) 01235 400454. Lines are open from 9.00–5.00,
Monday to Saturday, with a 24 hour message answering service. You can also order through
our website www.hoddereducation.co.uk

If you have any comments to make about this, or any of our other titles, please send them to
educationenquiries@hodder.co.uk

British Library Cataloguing in Publication Data
A catalogue record for this title is available from the British Library

ISBN: 978 1 444 14656 1

First Edition Published 2012

| Impression number | 10 9 8 7 6 5 4 3 2 1 |
| Year | 2015 2014 2013 2012 |

Copyright © 2012 Catherine Easton

Hachette UK's policy is to use papers that are natural, renewable and
recyclable products and made from wood grown in sustainable forests.
The logging and manufacturing processes are expected to conform to the
environmental regulations of the country of origin.

Cover photo © Anthony Baggett / iStockphoto.com
Typeset by Datapage India Pvt Ltd
Printed and bound in Spain for Hodder Education, An Hachette UK Company, 338 Euston
Road, London NW1 3BH

Contents

Guide to the book

Check new words and essential legal terms and what they mean

Definition

Capacity: understanding, awareness, capability, clear mind, reasoning, ability.

Test your legal knowledge! Practice makes perfect – answer questions on what you've just read

Workpoint

Why is capacity important in criminal law ?

Questions to help you delve deeper into the law and to guide your further reading

Research Point

In 2003 the Parliamentary Joint Committee on Human Rights criticised the age of criminal liability in their Tenth Report of Session 2002-03, HL1/High Court. Look up paragraphs 35 to 38 and make notes on the main arguments below.

Provides examples and extracts from the key cases and judgements you need to know

Case:	
Antoine (2000)	The words "did the act or made the omission" in the 1964 Act refer to the actus reus only. The mental element need not be explored.

Diagrams illustrate key points for visual learners

People who lack capacity in criminal law

Children under the age of ten

Corporations

Those with a mental illness

Tick off what you have learnt and check you're on track

Checkpoint - corporate manslaughter

I can explain the effect of *C v DPP* (1995) on the doctrine of doli incapax	
I can suggest ways in which a Crown Court trial could be made more accessible to a child.	

Provide you with potential real-life exam questions. Answers are available on the accompanying website.

Potential exam questions

1) Assess the ways in which incapacitated defendants are dealt with in the criminal court system

2) Examine the role of vicarious liability in criminal law

3) Corporations can be indicted for criminal offences the same as individuals can.

Guide to the website

There is useful additional material online to support your learning of law. Login at www.hodderplus.co.uk/law

Interactive questions to help you revise aspects of the law

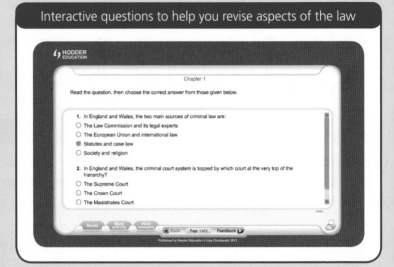

Model Answers

Chapter 1

1. When the criminal law prosecutes and sentences criminals, its purpose is to:

   • incapacitate the criminal

   • punish the criminal

   • deter the criminal and the public

   • reform the criminal

   • educate the criminal and the public

   • affirm moral standards and restore justice in society.

Useful links to websites to help you research further your studies in law

www.parliament.uk

The official Parliament website; use it to track all criminal bills currently before Parliament, explore the role of the House of Lords in law-making, and search for delegated legislation.

www.legislation.gov.uk

The official website for the Stationary Office; use it to search for newly enacted and revised legislation, draft legislation and statutory instruments for the United Kingdom, Scotland, Northern Ireland and Wales.

Acknowledgments

The author would like to thank Lucy Winder and Sundus Pasha for ensuring that the publication process progressed so smoothly.

Preface

The Course Notes series is intended to provide students with useful notes, which are presented in a way that helps with visual learning.

The series is also interactive with:

- Workpoints for students to work through

- Research Points where students are invited to further their knowledge and understanding by referring to important source materials

- Checkpoints to see whether the reader has understood/learned the key points on each topic

- Examination style questions at the end of each chapter.

There is also support available on the companion website where students can check their own answers to the examination-style questions against the suggested answers on the site, as well as interactive questions and useful links for research.

Jacqueline Martin

Course Notes: *The English Legal System*

A strong knowledge of the fundamentals of the English Legal System provides the essential backdrop of any English law course. The sources of the English Legal System and how they interact provide the context for further, detailed study in all areas of law. These are then placed alongside an understanding of the practicalities of the English Legal System with a focus on the court system, legal personnel and procedure. This text is an indispensable revision aid which succinctly and clearly provides the required English Legal System knowledge, making full use of current examples and diagrams. The workpoints and suggestions for further research guide students towards developing as independent learners and achieving their full potential, not only in English Legal System assessments but also in all future English legal study.

Catherine Easton

Table of cases

Table of statutes and other legislation

Chapter 1
Sources of Law

1.1 The English Legal System

The English legal system (ELS) draws upon the following sources:

- Common law: the law held in judges' decisions
- Equity: a source of law based on fairness
- Legislation: Acts of Parliament and secondary (delegated) legislation
- European Union law
- The European Convention on Human Rights.

1.2 Sources of Law

Who are the law-makers?

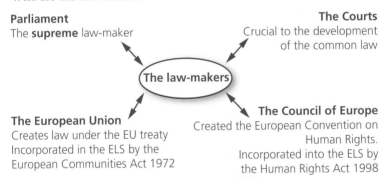

Parliament
The **supreme** law-maker

The Courts
Crucial to the development
of the common law

The law-makers

The European Union
Creates law under the EU treaty
Incorporated in the ELS by the
European Communities Act 1972

The Council of Europe
Created the European Convention on
Human Rights.
Incorporated into the ELS by
the Human Rights Act 1998

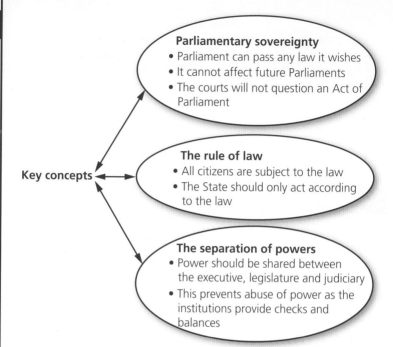

Parliamentary sovereignty
- Parliament can pass any law it wishes
- It cannot affect future Parliaments
- The courts will not question an Act of Parliament

Key concepts

The rule of law
- All citizens are subject to the law
- The State should only act according to the law

The separation of powers
- Power should be shared between the executive, legislature and judiciary
- This prevents abuse of power as the institutions provide checks and balances

1.3 The Courts

Supreme Court of the UK
(used to be House of Lords)
Hears appeals on civil and criminal law
(only on civil from Scotland)

Court of Appeal
Criminal division – hears appeals
Civil division – hears appeals

The High Court

Divisional Courts

Administrative Court	*Family Divisional*	*Chancery Divisional*
Hears judicial review and criminal appeals	Hears family appeals	Hears land and tax appeals

First Instance

Queen's Bench Division	*Family Division*	*Chancery Divisional*
Hears higher value civil claims	Hears family cases	Hears land/tax/trust cases

Figure continued overleaf

Crown Court
Hears criminal cases on indictment (see Chapter 5)

Magistrates' Court
Criminal trials/family
cases/bill non-payment

County Court
Lower value civil claims
family cases

Other Courts
Privy Council Hears issues relating to devolution and appeals from
the Commonwealth
The European Court of Justice (ECJ) See 1.7 below

Workpoint

Look at the diagram of the court system for five minutes, close the
book and then draw a very simple diagram of this system.

1.4 The Supreme Court of the UK

The House of Lords
Meaning 1: A chamber of Parliament: **still exists** to make law
alongside the House of Commons

~~The House of Lords~~
~~Meaning 2: The superior court in the English legal system~~

This has now been replaced…

Constitutional
Reform Act
2005

The Supreme Court
In October 2009 the Supreme Court of the UK replaced the House of
Lords as the superior court in the English legal system

Sources of law, hierarchy:

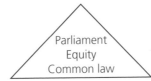

Parliament
Equity
Common law

1.5 The Common Law

The English legal system is said to be a common law system but the term 'common law' has a number of meanings:

- It can mean the law which applies to **all**.

- It can mean the law developed through judgments handed down in cases.

Example: murder is a 'common law' offence which is held in the judgments of key cases.

This aspect of the common law is underpinned by judicial precedent (see 2.1). It can mean the entire legal system of a country which operates in a similar way to the English legal system.

Contrast: civil law systems such as in Spain, which has its own extensive criminal and civil code and no doctrine of **binding** precedent. Remember this difference when studying judicial precedent.

It can relate to law which is not based in **equity**. To understand this difference, we need to understand **the historical development of English law**.

1.5.1 The development of the common law: a historical perspective

- Before 1066: there was no uniform law in the country.

- After 1066: a uniform, central system was developed with judges who travelled the country (named *Curia Regis*).

- This law applied to **all** (was 'common' to all).

- **But** if you did not lodge the correct paperwork (writ) then you could not have a remedy.

- **So** some people in this position took their case to **the King**.

- The King appointed a Lord High Chancellor to hear these cases in the Court of Chancery.

- The principles developed in this court became known as **equity**.

- The two court systems were fused together by the Judicature Acts 1873–75.

1.5.2 Equity today

- We know that the common law and equitable principles can now be administered in all courts.

- As equity was created to provide redress where there was none, it will prevail over the common law in case of conflict. An Act of Parliament would prevail over both of these sources (see 1.6).

- Equitable principles are based upon equality and fairness (you will study equity in more detail in, for example, the law of trusts).

- Equity has its own remedies, such as an injunction which can force or stop an act being performed.

- Equity will intervene where the law itself would produce absurd or unfair results.

> **Workpoint**
>
> Outline the differences between equity and the common law.

So, we know that the English legal system is a common law system within which laws are developed through judgments found in case law. We also know that within the court system equitable principles can be applied in the same courts alongside the common law. However, the highest source of law in the English legal system is Parliament and legislation.

1.6 Parliament and Legislation

Legislation can be split into two categories:

- **Primary**: Acts of Parliament, also known as statutes.

- **Secondary** or **delegated** or **subordinate**: This is where Parliament delegates law-making powers to, for example, a minister or a local authority (see below).

Parliament
- The House of Lords
- The House of Commons
- The Monarch

The majority of **primary** legislation (Acts of Parliament/statutes) is passed in the following way:

A proposal for a new law is drafted. This is known as a **Bill**.

There are different types of Bill. The first two apply to the country as a whole:

1. **Public Bills**: Bills drafted by the Government (the majority of Bills).

2. **Private Members' Bills**: Bills prepared by MPs who have been given the chance to propose a new law. Acts passed from Private Members' Bills include the Abortion Act 1967 and the Sustainable Communities Act 2007.

The final type of Bill usually applies only to the body who proposed it:

3. **Private Bills**: These are usually proposed by a body such as a large company or a local authority and usually only affect this actual organisation itself, e.g. the University of Manchester Act 2004.

Acts apply to country as a whole
Public Bills
Private Members' Bills

Acts usually apply **only** to the body who proposed it
Private Bills

Do not confuse Private Members' Bills with Private Bills. They may each have the word 'Private' in the title but when they become law, a Private Members' Bill will usually apply to **the country as a whole** whereas a Private Bill usually only impacts upon its proposer, e.g. a company/local authority.

A Bill can enter Parliament in either House (although the majority enter the House of Commons, financial or money Bills have to enter the House of Commons) and it goes through the following stages:

- First Reading
- Second Reading
- Committee Stage
- Report Stage
- Third Reading.

It is then passed to the other House where it goes through very similar stages and, if agreed upon, is sent for the Royal Assent to become law. Under the Parliament Acts of 1911–49, the Assent of the House of Lords may be bypassed under certain circumstances.

Royal Assent: **No Bill can become an Act without the Royal Assent.** Traditionally this means that the monarch must consent to the Bill becoming law. However, this is merely a formal process: the monarch does not read every Bill and give personal consent (it has not been withheld since 1707).

When does an Act come into force?

In force: Able to be relied upon in a court.

If a Bill has received the Royal Assent and become law, is it automatically in force? Answer: It depends upon its commencement.

Example: Section 29 of the Budget Responsibility and National Audit Act 2011 states:

Commencement

1. This Part comes into force on the day on which this Act is passed. *Therefore one Part comes into force on the day the Act received the Royal Assent (22nd March 2011).*

2. Section 27 and Schedule 6 come into force at the end of the period of two months beginning with the day on which this Act is passed. *Therefore these parts come into force on the date stated (22nd May 2011).*

3. The other provisions of this Act come into force in accordance with provision made by order made by statutory instrument by the Treasury. *The remaining sections will not come into force until a Minister in the Treasury makes a commencement order (a type of secondary legislation) to bring them into force.*

Therefore, an Act of Parliament does not automatically come into force on the day it receives the Royal Assent. You need to check its commencement.

Research Point

Locate an Act passed this month (either on paper or in a database) work out whether or not none, some, or all of it is in force.

Legislation – some statistics

In 2010:

41 UK Public General Acts (which apply to the country as a whole) were passed

5 UK Local Acts were passed

3,879 pieces of secondary or delegated legislation were passed

1.7 Secondary or Delegated Legislation

A **primary** Act of Parliament (statute) can pass on (delegate) power to another to make law. This is known as secondary or delegated legislation. The **primary** Act is known as the secondary (delegated) legislation's **parent** Act.

1.7.1 Types of secondary (delegated) legislation

1.7.1.1 Statutory instruments

A minister or government department can be given powers to commence an Act at a certain time. See above in relation to the commencement of the Budget Responsibility and National Audit Act 2011 – section 29(3) allows for the Treasury to bring certain sections into force.

Why are they used?

This allows for more specific, targeted control of the timing of an Act's sections coming into force in the light of evolving events without having to go back to Parliament.

1.7.1.2 By-laws

These are rules created by a public body such as a Local Authority.

Why are they used?

Would it be feasible for Parliament to set the specific rules which apply, for example, to parking in your local area? Would it be feasible for Parliament to, for example, set the specific fares and penalties which relate to your local transport network?

1.7.1.3 Orders in Council

These are a specific form of statutory instrument which are used in very important or urgent circumstances. They are officially made by the Legislative Committee of the Privy Council and can be used to respond to an emergency or enact domestic legislation.

Why are they used?

To allow a quick response to an emergency and to bring detailed rules into force.

Secondary (delegated) legislation is an important source of law and can affect many people in areas such as tax, immigration and health.

Advantages of secondary legislation

- Removes pressure on parliamentary time – this leaves more time for primary legislation to be debated.
- Speed – measures can be brought into force without having to go through the lengthy stages in Parliament.
- Expertise – complicated rules in areas such as tax can be created by, for example, Treasury representatives with technical expertise (which MPs may not have!).
- Local issues – a local authority will have a much better idea of the required measures in your local area.

Disadvantages of secondary legislation

- Scrutiny (technicalities) – due to the sometimes technical nature of secondary legislation, it can be difficult for MPs to understand the new measures.
- Scrutiny (amount of legislation) – due to the large amount of secondary legislation, it may be difficult for MPs to keep on top of new measures and understand their impact.
- Accountability – according to the theory of the separation of powers, the legislature (Parliament) should enact legislation. Increasing delegation of this power means that the law-making role is being shifted from Parliament and the processes may not be as accountable and open to scrutiny through public debate as primary legislation (this links to the two points above).

Due in part to the disadvantages listed above, a piece of secondary legislation can be struck down by a court if it is found to be *ultra vires* (beyond the powers) of its creator. The Parent Act (primary legislation) will outline the scope of the power to make secondary legislation and if its creator exceeds this power, then it can be struck down.

However, due to Parliamentary sovereignty, a piece of **primary** legislation **cannot** be struck down by a court.

Workpoint

Outline the differences between primary and secondary legislation and analyse the advantages and disadvantages of secondary legislation.

Research Point

Try to count all the by-laws which apply to your street or immediate local area. Find the full text of at least one of these and locate its parent Act and the section which delegates the powers to your local authority.

1.8 The European Union

Time line

1951 Early version of the European Union was created

1972 European Communities Act passed in the UK (key section: s 2)

1973 The UK joins the European Union (then Community)

1991 Case of *Factortame* (*No 2*): the House of Lords holds that if a statute and EU law conflict then the statute will be 'set aside' (**remember: not repealed**) and the EU law is applied

To clarify issues of EU law, the European Court of Justice (ECJ) hears references from the English legal system on matters of EU law. These references are **not appeals**.

The process

A domestic court has a case in which it needs advice on applying EU law

↓

It suspends the case and formulates a question or 'reference' to be submitted to the ECJ

↓

The ECJ answers the 'reference' and sends it back to the court in the English legal system

↓

The court applies the law following the reference provided by the ECJ and makes a decision on the case

1.9 The European Convention on Human Rights (ECHR)

This was created by the Council of Europe and enshrines key rights such as:

• Article 2: Right to Life

• Article 3: Prohibition of Torture.

The European Court of Human Rights (ECtHR) in Strasbourg makes decisions relating to the rights enshrined in the Treaty.

The Treaty was incorporated into the English legal system by the Human Rights Act 1998. The key change is that human rights principles as enshrined by the ECHR can now be relied on in UK courts; previously you had to appeal your case to the highest possible court (exhaust all domestic remedies) and then go to the ECtHR in Strasbourg. This took time and money.

Key sections of the Human Rights Act include:

s 2: When making a decision on a Convention issue the Court should take into account the past cases of the ECtHR (see Chapter 2)

s 3: Legislation should be interpreted in the light of the articles of the ECHR (see Chapter 3)

European Communities Act 1972

Section 2

(1) All such rights, powers, liabilities, obligations and restrictions from time to time created or arising by or under the Treaties, and all such remedies and procedures from time to time provided for by or under the Treaties, as in accordance with the Treaties are without further enactment to be given legal effect or used in the United Kingdom shall be recognised and available in law, and be enforced, allowed and followed accordingly; and the expression "enforceable EU right" and similar expressions shall be read as referring to one to which this subsection applies.

(4) ...any such provision (of any such extent) as might be made by Act of Parliament, and any enactment passed or to be passed, other than one contained in this part of this Act, shall be construed and have effect subject to the foregoing provisions of this section...

Human Rights Act 1998

Section 2

(1) A court or tribunal determining a question which has arisen in connection with a Convention right must take into account any—

(a) judgment, decision, declaration or advisory opinion of the European Court of Human Rights...

Section 3

(1) So far as it is possible to do so, primary legislation and subordinate legislation must be read and given effect in a way which is compatible with the Convention rights.

(2) This section—

(a) applies to primary legislation and subordinate legislation whenever enacted;

(b) does not affect the validity, continuing operation or enforcement of any incompatible primary legislation; and

(c) does not affect the validity, continuing operation or enforcement of any incompatible subordinate legislation if (disregarding any possibility of revocation) primary legislation prevents removal of the incompatibility.

1.10 Differences between the European Union and the European Convention on Human Rights

It is essential that you learn the differences between these two legal systems (they both have **Europe** in the title but are very different!).

	European Union	European Convention on Human Rights
Created	1951	1953
Key initial aims	Economic cohesion	Protection of human rights (post-WW2)
Nature	It creates law via institutions. These have a significant impact	This is static (no new laws are created)
Court	European Court of Justice	European Court of Human Rights
UK membership	Joined 1973	Ratified 1953
Key incorporating legislation and cases	European Communities Act 1972 s 2(1) and (4) *Factortame*	Human Rights Act 1998 ss 2, 3, 4 and 10 *R v A*
Impact of incorporation	If EU and UK law conflict, the UK statute will be set aside and the EU statute will be applied	If a UK statute conflicts with the ECHR, the judge could take a wide interpretation (s 3) taking into account past cases of the ECtHR (s 2) or make a Declaration of Incompatibility (s 4/s 10)

Workpoint

Briefly outline how a court would approach the following two imaginary scenarios:

A statute has been passed which states that people can no longer be housed in local authority care homes. Jane lives in a local authority care home and brings an action to state that the statute conflicts with her right to a family life.

continued overleaf

Workpoint (continued)

A statute governing working time has been passed which states that all hospital doctors can work 78 hours a week. The relevant EU law states that no doctors can be requested to work more than 70 hours a week. Tim is a hospital doctor who is routinely asked to work 78 hours a week. He brings an action, stating that the statute conflicts with EU law.

Checkpoint

Task	Done
I know the sources of the English legal system and can outline key concepts	
I can draw a simple diagram of the court system	
I understand the definitions of 'common law'	
I understand how equity developed and how it fits into the English legal system	
I know how Parliament makes law	
I know what delegated legislation is and can analyse its advantages and disadvantages	
I understand how the European Union impacts upon the English legal system	
I understand how the European Convention on Human Rights impacts upon the English legal system	
I know the difference between the European Union and the European Convention on Human Rights	

Potential exam questions

1) Outline, using examples, the sources of the English legal system.
2) Describe the process by which laws are made.
3) Outline the relationship between the courts of the English legal system and the European Court of Justice.
4) How has the English legal system incorporated the European Convention on Human Rights?

Chapter 2
The Doctrine of Judicial Precedent

2.1 What is the Doctrine of Judicial Precedent?

The English legal system follows the doctrine of judicial precedent. This relates to how past cases impact upon current cases.

Workpoint

Imagine that you are a solicitor advising Mr A, who has come to you to ask how he can claim damages from a building company who ruined his roof. Where do you start? A good place to look would be for other similar cases. You find the similar cases of Mr B and Ms C and start to build a case from there.

Some further issues:

In Mr B's case the builders ruined his conservatory, not his roof. Does this matter? Ms C's case is very similar to Mr A's but Ms C lost and was not awarded damages. Do you have to follow the legal principles in this case? Finally, where did you find out about Mr B's and Ms C's cases?

We will revisit these issues later but at this point need to state that following judicial precedent, certain cases **have to follow** the previous decisions of other courts. This is known as the principle of *stare decisis*.

Definition

Stare decisis: 'Stand by cases already decided'. When a legal principle has been decided in one case then this *has* to be followed in certain other courts.

Workpoint

Think back to Mr A above. What would be the point of developing the relevant legal principles from scratch when they have already been decided elsewhere?

Workpoint

Think about how a system could be developed in which this doctrine of judicial precedent based on *stare decisis* works effectively. Consider the following issues. How can the doctrine of judicial precedent function when there are thousands of cases heard every day – would there not be chaos? We've all read case reports and they're often very long! Does every single word impact upon other cases, and if so, how does any judge manage to make a decision?

To deal with these issues, the English legal system's doctrine of judicial precedent developed to require the following elements:

What is needed in a system which follows the doctrine of judicial precedent?

- A system of law reporting (so that we can find out how past legal principles were decided)

- A court hierarchy (so that only certain, important courts impact on others to avoid confusion)

- A method of working out exactly what the decided legal principle is (so that judges and lawyers can apply the law effectively). This legal principle is known as the *ratio decidendi*…

Definitions

Ratio decidendi: 'The reason for deciding'. The legal principle upon which a case is decided in the light of the material facts (it is the part of the case which is binding).

Material facts: The facts which are significant to the legal issue being decided in a case (they are the facts which matter!).

Example

Daisy Smith is an Australian citizen and is involved in two legal cases:

1. She sues Manchester City Council as she injured herself falling down an uncovered manhole.

2. She has been brought before an Immigration Tribunal in relation to her right to remain in the UK.

Workpoint

In which of these two cases would her Australian nationality be a material fact?

If the *ratio decidendi* is the binding legal principle found in a case, then what about the rest of the case? (Again, judicial decisions are often very long!) Words in a case which do not outline the reason why the decision was made are called *obiter dicta*.

Definition

Obiter dicta (plural)/*obiter dictum* (singular): 'Statements said by the way'/'A statement said by the way'. A statement or statements said in a case which do not form part of the *ratio decidendi* but can be **persuasive** (not binding!) in other cases. Examples include:

- A dissenting judgment (e.g. the minority decision in a Supreme Court case decided on a 4 in favour: 1 against basis).

- Legal discussion not directly related to the case itself.

- A hypothetical statement (e.g. in relation to Mr A's case above, the judge could say, '*If the contractors were plumbers, not builders, and broke a pipe then damages would be awarded on a different basis*').

These statements are not binding following *stare decisis* but they can be persuasive, e.g. if, after Mr A's case, another client came to you with a case in which a plumber broke a pipe, you could persuade a judge to follow the *obiter dictum* in Mr A's case in relation to plumbers. This, however, would not be **binding** as it did not form part of the *ratio decidendi*.

The higher the court, the more persuasive the *obiter dicta* will be. Remember this in relation to the court hierarchy discussed below.

A judgment can therefore be divided into its component parts:

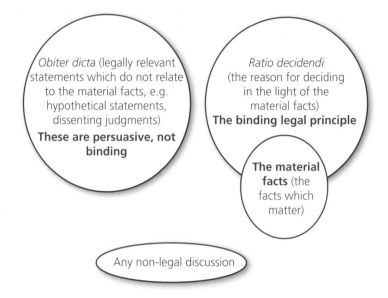

Obiter dicta (legally relevant statements which do not relate to the material facts, e.g. hypothetical statements, dissenting judgments) **These are persuasive, not binding**

Ratio decidendi (the reason for deciding in the light of the material facts) **The binding legal principle**

The material facts (the facts which matter)

Any non-legal discussion

Component parts of a judgment

Now we know that there is a method of extracting the binding legal principle, the *ratio decidendi*, from a case we need to examine how the courts interact with each other. To allow the doctrine of judicial precedent to function, a court hierarchy was developed. In order to understand how *stare decisis* works, some important points should be remembered:

• Superior courts bind lower courts. The lower courts **have** to follow the decisions of the higher courts. Lower courts **never** bind higher courts (although decisions can be persuasive).

Superior

Binding

Inferior

Superior

Never binding

Inferior

• The rules governing whether or not a court binds itself are specific to each court. They will be discussed below.

• *Stare decisis* is applied more strictly in civil rather than criminal cases.

Workpoint

Can you determine why this might be the case? We will revisit this below.

2.2 The Court Hierarchy

This is a simplified diagram of the court system which highlights how the system of precedent operates. The points relating to whether a court binds itself will be discussed in greater detail below.

**Superior courts
bind those below**

Court	Does it bind itself?
Supreme Court	Usually follows its own decisions but since the Practice Statement of 1966 is free to depart
Court of Appeal Civil Division/Criminal Division	Usually follows its own decisions subject to the exceptions in *Young v Bristol Aeroplane*. The criminal division is slightly more flexible
High Court Administrative Court — Family Divisional — Chancery Divisional Judicial Review and Appeals — Appeals — Appeals	As these are appeals, they follow the rules in *Young v Bristol Aeroplane*, the same as the Court of Appeal
Queen's Bench Division — Family Division — Chancery Division	These courts are not bound following strict *stare decisis* but past decisions are **very** persuasive
Crown Court	Merely persuasive
County Court — **Magistrates' Court**	Neither binding nor persuasive

A simplified diagram of the court system

Some issues relating to the courts and precedent are discussed in more detail below.

2.3 How the Doctrine Applies to Individual Courts

2.3.1 The Supreme Court and the Practice Statement

Since October 2009, the House of Lords was replaced by the Supreme Court (see below, and Chapters 4 and 5 for more detail).

The approach to precedent in the House of Lords now applies to the Supreme Court.

1898: *London Tramways Co Ltd v London County Council* [1898] AC 375: The House of Lords stated that it was strictly bound by its past decisions.

$\downarrow$

1966: Practice Statement [1966] 3 All ER 77 (not a case but a statement of how the court regulates itself): '*... Their Lordships ... propose therefore to modify their present practice and, while treating former decisions of this House as normally binding, to depart from a previous decision when it appears right to do so.*'

So is the Supreme Court bound by its past decisions or not? Looking at the Practice Statement, the Supreme Court considers itself normally bound but will depart when it appears right to do so. When is this? No extra guidance was given on this point.

We can learn more by looking at the Lords' reasons for not departing from past decisions. In the case of *Jones v Secretary of State for Social Services* (1972) 1 All ER 145, the majority of the Law Lords decided that a past precedent relating to the interpretation of a statute was wrong but refused to depart from it. It was stated that the Practice Statement should **not** be used when:

- The previous case involved incorrect statutory interpretation.
- No wider issues of public policy are involved.
- It should be Parliament that legislates to change the law.
- Departing would cause uncertainty.
- The decision was merely wrong.

To analyse this further, we need to investigate some examples of the rare times when the court **has** used the power to depart from past decisions:

Case	Subject area	Reason for departing
Conway v Rimmer (1968) departed from *Duncan v Cammell Laird & Co* (1942)	Public interest immunity	Changes in society (the previous precedent was laid down during the Second World War)
Herrington v British Railways Board (1972) departed from *Addie & Sons v Dumbreck* (1929)	Landowners' duties to trespassers	Society's views had developed to be more disposed to protecting the rights of trespassers, particularly children
Murphy v Brentwood Borough Council (1991) departed from *Anns v Merton Borough Council* (1978)	Negligence in relation to the inspection of building foundations	Bringing clarity to a legal principle which was deemed to have widened too far
Miliangos v George Frank (Textiles) Ltd (1975) departed from *Re United Railways of Havana* (1960)	The currency in which damages should be awarded	Changes in society and economics, there was no acceptable reason to always award damages in sterling
R v Shivpuri (1986) departed from *Anderton v Ryan* (1985)	The law relating to criminal attempts	The previous decision was merely wrong! Note the proximity in the dates. Note also the issues discussed in the *Jones* case above
R v G (2003) departed from *R v Caldwell* (1982)	The definition of recklessness in certain crimes	The law desperately needed clarification and the principles in *Caldwell* had led to some very harsh decisions (e.g. a girl with learning difficulties was judged on objective standards – *Elliott v C* (1983)).

2.3.1.1 Some issues

The Practice Statement noted the danger of '*disturbing retrospectively the basis on which contracts, settlements of property and fiscal arrangements have been entered into.*'

As we saw above, the doctrine of precedent relies upon superior courts making a small number of important decisions which are then followed by courts lower in the hierarchy. If the Supreme Court often changes the legal principles relating to, for example, contract terms, then those entering into long-term negotiations would not know which law would apply to them (their legitimate expectations would be affected). Lawyers would not know how to advise their clients.

The Practice Statement also highlighted '*the especial need for certainty as to the criminal law*'. Citizens and those applying the criminal law need to be clear exactly what constitutes a crime and a defence. However, note the criminal case of *R v Shivpuri* which departed from a decision of one year earlier relating to the Criminal Attempts Act 1981. The nature of a specific crime changed in one year and this had to trickle down the court hierarchy.

Workpoint

Do you believe that the need for the law to be correct outweigh the need for certainty?

The arguments for and against the existence of the Practice Statement often fall into two camps:

Flexibility	v	Certainty
The law needs to update as society updates (see *Miliangos*)		The hierarchy of the courts and judicial precedent operate on the basis that the superior courts with the best judges make definitive decisions
Incorrect decisions need to be changed to avoid injustice (see *Shivpuri*)		The best judges in the country should not make mistakes. If they know they have the Practice Statement then they might take their decisions less seriously
There is a need to bring clarity to certain legal areas (see *R v G*)		There is a need for certainty in the criminal law and legitimate expectations are essential to contract law

2.3.2 The Court of Appeal and Judicial Precedent

This Court is bound by the decisions of the superior court, the Supreme Court.

The Court of Appeal (CA) is bound by its past decisions subject to the exceptions outlined in the case of *Young v Bristol Aeroplane Co Ltd* [1944] 2 All ER 293. These are:

1. Where two previous decisions of the Court of Appeal conflict with each other. This can occur when decisions are made at a similar time. In this case the later court can choose which precedent to follow, e.g.:

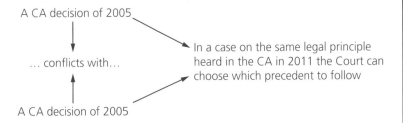

A CA decision of 2005

... conflicts with...

A CA decision of 2005

In a case on the same legal principle heard in the CA in 2011 the Court can choose which precedent to follow

2. Where a previous Court of Appeal decision conflicts with a subsequent Supreme Court decision, the later court **must** follow the Supreme Court decision, e.g.:

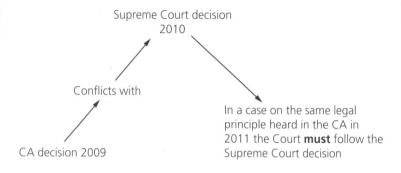

Supreme Court decision
2010

Conflicts with

CA decision 2009

In a case on the same legal principle heard in the CA in 2011 the Court **must** follow the Supreme Court decision

3. Where the previous Court of Appeal decision was decided *per incuriam* then the Court of Appeal will not be bound to follow it, e.g.:

Binding CA decision 2008

If the Court of Appeal in 2011 finds the past decision to be *per incuriam* it will not be bound to follow its *ratio decidendi*

Definition

Per incuriam: 'Through lack of care'. If the judgment overlooked either a binding precedent or relevant statutory provision and, due to this, the final decision was incorrect.

The case of *Williams v Fawcett* (1985) 1 All ER 787 extended this definition to apply in cases when:

• The mistake is easy to determine

• The case concerns individual liberty

• There is likely to be no further route of appeal.

2.3.3 Issues relating the Court of Appeal (Criminal Division)

It was stated above that strict adherence to *stare decisis* can be relaxed in criminal cases. This is because criminal cases can have severe implications for the liberty of individuals.

It is accepted that the Court of Appeal (Criminal Division) will be more flexible in relation to judicial precedent than the Court of Appeal (Civil Division).

In the case of *R v Simpson* (2003) EWCA Crim 1499, Lord Woolf CJ stated that in relation to the Court of Appeal (Criminal Division):

- Precedent can be followed in a less rigid manner, particularly if there is likely to be no right to appeal.

- Judges should be very aware of the consequences of strict adherence to *stare decisis*.

2.3.4 The High Court, Divisional Courts and Judicial Precedent

These courts are bound by the decisions of the superior courts; the Supreme Court and the Court of Appeal.

The Divisional Courts of the High Court hear appeals and follow the same approach as the Court of Appeal. That is:

- They are normally bound by their past decisions.

- They are subject to the three exceptions in *Young v Bristol Aeroplane Ltd*.

- There is more flexibility in criminal cases (heard in the Queen's Bench Divisional Court, also known as the Administrative Court).

2.3.4.1 The High Court

- This court is bound by the decisions of all courts higher than it.

- The High Court hears cases at first instance.

- It is not strictly bound by its own past decisions but these are highly persuasive.

2.3.4.2 The Crown Court

- This court is bound by the decisions of all courts higher than it.

- It is not strictly bound by its own past decisions but these are persuasive.

2.3.4.3 The County Courts and Magistrates' Courts

- These courts are bound by all courts above them.

- These courts do not bind themselves (this would be very difficult in relation to court reporting).

- The decisions of these courts bind no other courts.

2.4 Precedent and the Human Rights Act 1998

Throughout this examination of precedent and the hierarchy of the courts, it has been stated that lower courts are **bound** by superior courts.

However, the Human Rights Act s 2(1) places a duty on inferior courts to avoid precedent if the superior court's decision is not compatible with a decision taken by the European Court of Human Rights.

This duty was exercised in the case of *Mendoza v Ghaidan* [2004] UKHL 30 in which the Court of Appeal avoided a binding House of Lords precedent which was not compatible with the European Convention on Human Rights.

Workpoint

In the case of a conflict between the common law principles of *stare decisis* and a statute, namely the Human Rights Act 1998, following what was learned in Chapter 1 about sources of law, can you determine which takes precedence and why?

2.5 The Declaratory Theory

The declaratory theory outlined by William Blackstone states judges simply **declare** the law, they do not **make** the law. Only Parliament **makes** the law.

Following this, if a decision is overruled it is deemed never to have existed, e.g.:

> Trust Law decision 1, 2000
>
> A trust is created, 2004
>
> Trust Law decision 2, 2011 overrules Trust Law decision 1
>
> When a case involving the trust created in 2004 comes to court in 2011, it will be judged on the law as it is in 2011, not 2004 when it was created

However, the declaratory theory is not realistic as certain key legal principles such as negligence developed through the common law and were not created by Parliament.

It can be said that judges, within the constraints of the doctrine of precedent outlined above, do have some discretion in relation to the decisions they make and can impact on the law's development. Lord Reid said that where there is some discretion in relation to a decision, judges should have regard to (in this order):

1. Common sense

2. Legal principle

3. Public policy.

However, does judicial discretion not undermine Parliament's role as the supreme law-maker and the separation of powers? This area links to sources of law in Chapter 1 and statutory interpretation in Chapter 3.

Workpoint

To what extent do you agree with the statement 'judges make law'?

2.6 Avoiding Precedents

Throughout this chapter we have discussed *stare decisis*, the doctrine of **binding** precedent. However, what happens if you are advising a client and the court following a **binding** precedent in a previous case would lead to your client losing?

Remember Mr A's case at the very beginning of the chapter? It was stated that Ms C's case is very similar to Mr A's but Ms C lost and was not awarded damages. Do you have to follow the legal principles in this case?

Following strict *stare decisis*, the answer would be **yes**. However, remember the definition of *ratio decidendi*: it is 'the legal principle upon which a case is decided in the light of the **material facts**'.

If it can be proved that key facts in Mr A's case are sufficiently different from Ms C's (if, for example, Mr A's building was domestic and Ms C's building was commercial), then the binding precedent can be avoided. This is known as **distinguishing**.

Definition

Distinguishing: The process by which a past binding precedent is avoided by proving that its material facts were sufficiently different.

Distinguishing therefore can lessen the impact of the rigid nature of *stare decisis* and can give the law space to develop.

Courts can also **reverse** a decision.

> ### Definition
>
> Reverse: Where a higher court reaches a different decision from a lower court as **the same case** travels up the court hierarchy.

For example, let's consider a hypothetical case of *Smith v Jones*.

2nd Appeal: Court of Appeal (Civil Division)	Court finds for Smith **Decision is reversed (again)**
	↑
1st Appeal: High Court Queen's Bench Divisional Court	Court finds for Jones **Decision is reversed**
	↑
First Instance: County Court	Court finds for Smith

> ### Definition
>
> Overrule: Where a higher court states that a lower court's decision **in a different case** is wrong and no longer good law. This extinguishes the precedent value of the lower court's decision.

The Supreme Court and Court of Appeal can also **overrule** a past precedent. This involves **more than one case** eg:

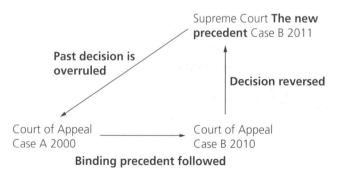

Checkpoint

Task	Done
I can define the doctrine of judicial precedent	
I can outline the necessary requirements for the doctrine to function	
I can define the different elements of a judgment	
I know how courts bind each other in the court hierarchy	
I know the rules relating to how courts bind themselves	
I can analyse the advantages and disadvantages of precedent	
I understand the impact the Human Rights Act 1998 has had on judicial precedent	
I can outline and evaluate the declaratory theory	
I can define the terms distinguishing, reversing and overruling	

Potential exam questions

1) To what extent do judges make law?
2) What are the essential ingredients in a system of judicial precedent?
3) Explain why it is important to distinguish between *ratio decedendi* and *obiter dictum*.
4) Draw a diagram of the court hierarchy.
5) Explain, with reference to case law examples, the effect of the Practice Statement of 1966.
6) Is the Court of Appeal bound by its own previous decisions?

Chapter 3
Statutory Interpretation

3.1 Introduction

As we saw in Chapter 1, a statute created by Parliament is the highest form of law in the English legal system. Following the doctrine of the separation of powers, all judges should do is **apply** the law created by Parliament. Remember:

Government (Executive) **proposes** the law

Parliament (Legislature) **enacts** the law

Judges (Judiciary) **apply** the statute independently to give light to the aim of Parliament

- Statutes are in essence rules.

- These rules are expressed in words.

- Judges should therefore find it easy to interpret statutes and do their job. However…

Imagine a law controlling access to parks stating: '*Men with beards or moustaches cannot enter public parks*'. Would a man with both a moustache **and** a beard be allowed in? Does the statute, reading it literally, actually refer to him?

Workpoint

Put yourself in the place of the judge in the following hypothetical cases and say how you would decide them.

The defendant was caught bombarding a large commercial website with emails which eventually took the site offline temporarily. The relevant statute on hacking makes it illegal to 'modify or damage' a computer system. Guilty or not guilty?

A statute may be drafted in a way which does not foresee potential technological developments.

The defendant was caught smuggling a highly addictive hallucinogenic drug, Oxi, into the UK. The relevant statute has a list of substances which are very similar to Oxi but it is not specifically referred to in the statute. Guilty or not guilty?

A statute may not be able to cover all possible circumstances.

Under equality legislation, service providers are 'required to make their services accessible to disabled people'. A case is brought against a large airline claiming that they have a duty to provide a website which is accessible to disabled people using assistive technology. Is the website a service?

A statute may be drafted too broadly to be sufficiently clear.

The defendant was caught riding an electric bicycle at 30 miles an hour on a pavement. The relevant statute bans 'vehicles' on pavements, the definition of 'vehicle' specifically includes 'moped and motorcycles' but excludes 'bicycles'. Guilty or not guilty?

Certain terms can be ambiguous even with further clarification.

Those who draft legislation are simply human and can sometimes get things wrong. Try to relate this back to what you know about the process by which a Bill becomes an Act and the many stages it goes through, with many amendments made.

If the role of the judge is simply to apply the law to give light to the aim of Parliament and this is difficult to determine, then what does a judge do?

If he or she looks beyond the statute, is this not 'making law' and undermining the role of Parliament?

If the statute is clear the judge ⟶ **Interprets the law**

If there is an ambiguity in the statute the judge ⟶ **Constructs (determines the meaning of) the law**

3.2 The Three 'Rules'

So how do judges approach statutes? Three 'rules' have been identified:

1. The literal rule
2. The golden rule
3. The mischief rule.

Ironically, in this context the word 'rule' is ambiguous. These are more like 'approaches'; they do not constrain judges, judges can choose to follow these approaches as they wish.

As Lord Reid states: 'They are not rules in the ordinary sense of having some binding force. They are our servants, not our masters. They are aids to construction, presumptions or pointers. Not infrequently one "rule" points in one direction, another in a different direction. In each case we must look at all relevant circumstances and decide as a matter of judgment what weight to attach to any particular "rule".' (*Maunsell v Olins* (1975)

Definition

The literal rule: Give the words their plain, ordinary meaning even if this leads to a result which does not seem to make sense.

Case:	
***Whiteley v Chappell* (1868)**	The relevant statute made it a crime to impersonate people 'entitled to vote'. The defendant impersonated a dead person. The court found that as dead people cannot vote the defendant was not guilty.

Do you agree with this result?

Definition

The golden rule: This builds upon the literal rule. The words of the statute are given their plain, ordinary meaning but if this results in an absurdity, then the statute can be interpreted to avoid this absurdity. This approach can be **narrow** – where a word has more than one meaning, choose the one which avoids the absurdity.

Case:	
R v Allen (1872)	The defendant married a woman while his first wife was still alive. The relevant statute stated: '*Whosoever, being married, shall marry any other person during the lifetime of his spouse shall commit an offence*'.
	Any bigamous marriage is automatically void *ab initio*, i.e. never a marriage at all. Had the defendant committed an offence in marrying another woman whilst his wife was still living? Answer: no, as the second marriage never existed in the eyes of the law. The court decided that 'marry' could also mean 'go through the ceremony of marriage' to find that defendant guilty.

The second approach can be **wide** where the words of the statutes are modified to avoid the absurdity (this is similar to the purposive approach below).

Case:	
Re Sigsworth (1935)	A son murdered his mother. The mother did not leave a will. The statute stated that where there was not a will, the next of kin would inherit. This was the son, as her 'issue'. On a literal interpretation, the son would inherit, but the court found this repugnant and took a 'golden rule' approach to interpret the statute to state that an 'issue' could not inherit when he or she had killed the benefactor.

Workpoint

Consider whether you believe this is an example of judges going beyond their powers and 'making law'. If Parliament had wanted this result, would it not have included it in the statute? However, is it likely that Parliament did not foresee such a situation?

The mischief rule: This is also known as the rule in *Heydon's Case* (1584). Following this approach, the judge will:

1. Determine what the common law was before the Act was passed.

2. Identify a mischief (i.e. what was wrong with the common law that Parliament sought to remedy with the passing of the Act).

3. Assume that Parliament created the Act to address this mischief and interpret the statute in the light of this.

Case:	
Smith v Hughes (1960)	The Street Offences Act 1959 made it an offence to *'loiter or solicit in a street or public place'*. The defendants in question had solicited by standing on balconies and calling for attention from behind half-open or closed windows. On a literal interpretation, would they be guilty? The court determined that the mischief was the molestation of people on the streets and interpreted the statute in the light of this to find the defendants guilty.

If all judges have is the words of the statute, then how do they identify the mischief? Is this not second guessing Parliament?

In the past, Acts were published with preambles which often outlined what was wrong with the common law before the Act was passed. See 3.7 for more on intrinsic aids to interpretation.

3.3 The Purposive Approach

More recently a new approach has developed, influenced by the UK's membership of the European Union. In Chapter 1 we highlighted the difference between common law and civil law systems. Many European countries and the European Union itself take a purposive approach to interpretation as the ultimate mechanism of legal interpretation upon failure of the grammatical/literal approach.

Definition

The purposive approach: Interpret the law in the light of its wider general aims and principles. This particularly applies when interpreting a statute in the light of EU law. However, this approach is becoming increasingly more common throughout the English legal system.

Case:	
***R v Registrar General, ex p Smith* (1991)**	The applicant was a convicted murderer detained in a high security psychiatric hospital who wanted to obtain his birth certificate and learn the identity of his mother. The relevant statute stated that the Registrar General 'shall… supply' the documentation. It was determined that the applicant could pose a danger to his mother. The judges took a wide approach, looking at the general aims of the statute and decided that Parliament could not have intended to promote serious crime. Therefore, despite the words of the statute, they ruled that the Registrar did not have to supply the birth certificate.

Again is this not the judges 'making law' and second guessing Parliament. How do they know the general aims of the statute?

Research Point

Increasingly statutes are published with Explanatory Notes which may outline the general aims of the law. Find an Act which has Explanatory Notes and determine to what extent you believe they are useful in the interpretation of the aims of the Act.

Text-based approaches	Contextual approaches
These focus on the words	These look beyond the act
The literal rule – give the words their plain and ordinary meaning. For example, *Whiteley v Chappell*	**The mischief rule**
However, if this leads to an absurdity then the judge may use…	Look to the common law **before** the Act, identify the mischief it was passed to remedy. Interpret the statute in the light of this mischief. For example, *Smith v Hughes*
The golden rule For example, *R v Allen; Re Sigsworth*	**The purposive approach**
Narrow Choose most suitable meaning of a word	**Wide** Modify the words	Look to the wider general aims of the Act and determine what Parliament sought to achieve **in the future**. Interpret the statute in the light of this. For example, *R v Registrar General; exp Smith*

3.4 Evaluating the Rules

Text-based approaches
(Literal and Golden Rules)

Pros of text-based approaches
• Allow judges to fulfil their constitutional role of simply applying the law.
• All judges should do is apply the words of Acts, it is for Parliament to change these words if there is an absurdity.
• Statutes are rules, rules are made up of words, all the judges have is the words, this is all they should apply.

Cons of text-based approaches
• Can lead to absurd results (see *Whiteley v Chappell*).
• Statutes may be ambiguous, out-of-date, too broad or incorrectly drafted.
• The golden rule is too vague and therefore dangerous.
• If statutes are clear and the words easy to apply, then why do we need judges at all, couldn't computers do the job just as well?

Figure continued overleaf

Contextual approaches
(Mischief Rule and Purposive Approach)

Pros

- Words may not always express intention; there is a need to look beyond words to give light to the intention Parliament effectively.
- Allows judges to use their expertise to avoid absurdities to come to the result that Parliament would have intended.
- The purposive approach is a more modern approach to statutory interpretation and puts us more in line with European countries and the EU.

Cons

- Give judges far too much power and allows them to second guess the intention of Parliament and 'make law'.
- How do judges know what Parliament's intention is? There are some extrinsic aids to interpretation (see below) but these themselves require interpretation.
- When do judges decide to look at the context of the Act–always? When the result does not match their own notion of what is correct?

3.5 Rules of Language

At the beginning of the chapter, the difficulties of drafting an effective statutory provision were noted. Due to this, a number of legislative shortcuts have been identified to aid the drafting and interpreting of legislation. These are:

- *Ejusdem generis*
- *Expression unius est exclusion alterius*
- *Noscitur a sociis*.

Definition

> *Ejusdem generis*: 'Of the same kind'. General words are to be interpreted as being of the same kind as specific ones which come before them. There needs to be more than one specific word. We interpret the general terms according to the 'common and dominant' characteristics of the specific words.

Case:	
***Powell v Kempton Park Racecourse* (1899)**	The statute prohibited keeping a 'house, office, room or other place for betting'. In this case the 'place' was outdoors. Was it covered by the statute? Answer: no, as the specific places referred to in the statute are all indoors.

This rule of language is the most commonly used. It allows a statute to cover similar situations or areas which may not have been foreseen at the time of drafting. Looking back to the activity at the beginning relating to the drug 'Oxi', a specific list of drugs followed by the words 'and other similar substances' may have been able to catch this substance even though it was unknown at the time of drafting.

Workpoint

Create your own example of the use of *ejusdem generis* and try to determine how to interpret the general words. For example, '*fridges, cookers, toasters and other household appliances*'. Would an alarm clock fall into the general category? A hairdryer? A kettle?

Definition

Expressio unius est exclusio alterius: 'The mention of one thing excludes others.' Where there is a closed set of words, then the statute **only** applies to those words and no others.

Case:	
Tempest v Kilner (1846)	The statute applied to 'goods, wares and merchandise', therefore it did not apply to stocks and shares. They were simply not mentioned on the closed list.

This rule demonstrates why *ejusdem generis* is often used to provide a 'catch all' in case of future developments.

Definition

Noscitur a sociis: 'A word is known by the company it keeps.' Interpret a term in the light of words which accompany it.

Case:	
Foster v Diphwys Casson Slate Co (1887)	The statute covered a 'case or canister'. The court had to determine whether a cloth bag was a 'case' and decided it was not, as the word's company was 'canister' and this denoted a hard carrier, not a soft one such as a cloth bag.

Think of words which can have different meanings in different contexts. For example, 'a match'. In context it can mean different things, e.g. 'match and lighter' or 'match and game'.

3.6 Presumptions

When judges interpret any statute, they do so in the light of certain accepted presumptions. Presumptions do not have to be followed if a statute specifically goes against it (rebuts it).

Some presumptions are illustrated below:

Against change to the common law
Any change to the common law should be **expressly** stated in a statute.

***Mens rea* is needed in criminal cases**
A defendant should only be found guilty if they have the required mental state for the crime.

Against binding the Crown (the State)
If a statute does not **expressly** state that the Crown is bound then it is not. The presumption is rebutted in, for example, the Equal Pay Act 1970 which specifically binds the Crown.

Against retrospective application of legislation
Imagine if a statute is passed today which makes it illegal to own a mobile phone but states that this applies to the 12 months prior to it coming into force. Would you be a criminal? Is this fair?
Statutes do not usually apply to things that that happened before they came into force. This presumption is rebutted in, for example, the War Damage Act 1965. Remember this area when you study parliamentary sovereignty in public law.

Against legislating in a manner incompatible with the ECHR and the EU treaties
The UK operates under its international duties and it is presumed that Parliament will not seek to create statutes which conflict with obligations entered into under the ECHR and the EU treaties.

3.7 Intrinsic and Extrinsic Aids to Interpretation

Remember that the role of judges is to give light to the intention of Parliament. To do so they can consult certain accepted sources.

3.7.1 Intrinsic (internal) aids

These are part of the Act itself and include:

- Long title

- Short title

- Preamble (note: remember how this could aid the mischief rule)

- Headings

- Schedules.

Marginal notes are not the words of Parliament and merely help in the navigation of the statute; they therefore should not be used as an aid to interpretation.

3.7.2 Extrinsic (external) aids

These are found outside of the statute itself. Remember issues relating to the separation of powers and how judges should simply apply the words of a statute.

These include:

- Previous Acts of Parliament on the same topic

- The historical setting

- Earlier case law

- Contemporary dictionaries

- The Interpretation Act 1978 – this includes rules such as 'he' includes 'she' and singular includes plural.

Other extrinsic aids to interpretation are as follows.

3.7.3 Explanatory notes

- Since 1998, Bills are printed with Explanatory Notes.

- These are not part of the Act.

• There is no definitive rule as to whether these can be used but, for example, in the Fraud Act 2006, the Government allowed an important principle to be included in the Explanatory Notes and not the Act itself.

Workpoint

Which rule(s) to statutory interpretation would make use of Explanatory Notes and which would not?

3.7.4 Hansard

Definition

Hansard: An official word-for-word record of what is said in the proceedings and debates in Parliament.

Research Point

Access Hansard online at www.parliament.uk/business/publications/hansard/. Find a debate on a recent Bill. Determine who was the proposer of the Bill. What reading of the Bill have you found? Are the statements clear?

Workpoint

Can you think of how Hansard could be useful to a judge trying to interpret a statute in which there is a perceived absurdity?

3.7.4.1 Hansard timeline

Pre 1978: Rule that the courts **cannot** look at Hansard to help in statutory interpretation

1978: *Davis v Johnson* (1978)
Denning strongly criticises this rule. Admits: '*I do it anyway*'

1992: *Pepper v Hart* (1993)
The rule against the use of Hansard is relaxed in the following circumstances:

• When a statute is found to be ambiguous; and
• The statement in Hansard is made by the relevant minister or promoter of the Bill; and
• This statement is clear.

3.7.4.2 Use of Hansard

Points in favour:
- If it is only used in the specified circumstances to resolve a specific ambiguity, then it sheds light on Parliament's intention and helps judges to do their job.
- Denning: *'Why grope in the dark when you can switch on the lights?'*
- Denning: Judges do this anyway, the process should be formalised.

Points against:
- Blurs the separation of powers: judges look beyond the statute and second-guess Parliament.
- Using Hansard increases the cost and duration of legal cases.
- Hansard is merely words – these words will also need interpretation!
- Do Parliamentary debates fully represent the views of Parliament? Shouldn't statutes do this?

3.7.5 Law Reform Reports

These could not be used until 1975 (decided in *Black-Clawson International Ltd v Papierwerke* etc. (1975).

In *Black-Clawson* it was stated they could be used to determine the mischief a statute was passed to remedy. However, *Pepper v Hart* clarifies that they can be used to determine Parliament's intention.

Some cases in which the courts have not referred to Law Reform Reports for clarification have been criticised, e.g. *R v Caldwell* (1981) and *Anderton v Ryan* (1985) (remember these cases in relation to judicial precedent in Chapter 2).

3.7.6 International conventions

Where a statute has been passed to give effect to an international convention, this can be referred to in order to interpret it (e.g. *Salomon v Commissioners of Customs and Excise* (1966).

In *Fothergill v Monarch Airlines Ltd* (1980), it was held that even preparatory material and explanatory notes relating to the convention could be consulted.

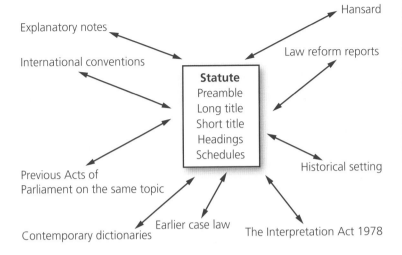

3.8 The Impact of the Human Rights Act 1998

Section 3 of the Human Rights Act 1998 states: '*So far as it is possible to do so, primary legislation and subordinate legislation must be read and given effect in a way which is compatible with the Convention rights*'.

Therefore when interpreting a statute, judges should, 'so far as it is possible', choose the interpretation which leads to the result that is more compatible with the European Convention on Human Rights (ECHR) than any other.

Case:	
***Mendoza v Ghaidan* (2004)**	The approach was taken to interpret the words 'as his or her wife or husband' to apply to a same-sex couple, achieving a result which was more compatible with the ECHR.

Case:	
***R v A* (2001)**	Lord Steyn: the interpretation can even be '*linguistically strained*' to achieve compatibility with the ECHR.

Workpoint

Analyse whether or not you believe that the Human Rights Act has given judges too much power to make creative decisions.

Checkpoint

Task	Done
I know why statutory interpretation is needed	
I know the three rules to statutory interpretation and can give examples of their use	
I understand the purposive approach and can give examples of its use	
I can evaluate the advantages and disadvantages of the rules	
I understand the rules of language and when they are used	
I know which intrinsic and extrinsic aids to interpretation can be used	
I know the arguments for and against the use of Hansard	
I know how the Human Rights Act 1998 has impacted statutory interpretation	

Potential exam questions

1) Explain, with reference to case law examples, which you believe to be the most effective rule of statutory interpretation.
2) What are the advantages and disadvantages of a contextual approach to statutory interpretation?
3) Define, using examples, the following rules of construction:
   - *Ejusdem generis*
   - *Expression uniusest exclusion alterius*
   - *Noscitur a sociis*.
4) What are the presumptions of statutory interpretation?
5) What was the impact of the case of *Pepper v Hart* on the interpretation of statutes?

Chapter 4
Civil Courts

4.1 Introduction to the Courts System

A detailed knowledge of the courts system underpins the doctrine of judicial precedent as outlined in Chapter 2.

Remember that:

- Whether a case's subject matter is **criminal** or **civil** will decide which court hears a case.

- Some courts are higher than others, e.g. the Supreme Court is higher than the Magistrates' Court. Try to link this back into your understanding of *stare decisis*.

- Some courts hear cases for the first time (**trial courts**) some hear cases on appeal (**appellate courts**).

- There is also a system of tribunals covering certain legal areas.

4.1.1 Civil and criminal cases

If the court in which a case is heard is determined by whether it is civil or criminal we need to examine the differences between **civil** and **criminal** law:

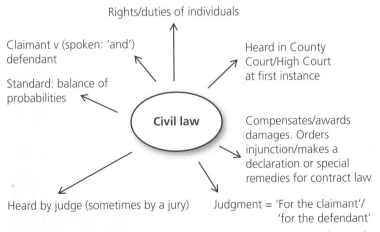

Rights/duties of individuals

Claimant v (spoken: 'and') defendant

Standard: balance of probabilities

Heard in County Court/High Court at first instance

Civil law

Compensates/awards damages. Orders injunction/makes a declaration or special remedies for contract law

Heard by judge (sometimes by a jury)

Judgment = 'For the claimant'/ 'for the defendant'

Some branches of civil law: land law, employment law, company law and the law of tort

Criminal law

- Regulates behaviour, determines guilt, imposes penalty
- Defendant is prosecuted by the state through Crown Prosecution Service
- Heard in Magistrates' Court/Crown Court at first instance
- Standard: beyond reasonable doubt
- Decisions made by magistrates or jury
- R (the State) v (spoken: 'against') defendant
- Judgment = Guilty/not guilty
- Sentences include imprisonment/fines/community sentences (compensation can also be awarded)

Workpoint

In each of the following short scenarios outline whether or not the case would be criminal or civil or both and then state:

- Who would bring the case.

- The standard of proof.

- The potential outcome of the case.

    1. Mr Blyth has been unfairly dismissed from his job.

    2. Mr Blyth got into a fight in a bar and punched a man in the face.

    3. Mr Blyth was driving without paying full attention and crashed into a car causing whiplash injuries to the two passengers.

Workpoint

Consider why the standard of proof is different for civil and criminal cases.

4.1.2 Superior courts and inferior courts

Workpoint

Before studying this section take a look back at the simple diagram of the court hierarchy at 2.2.

Superior courts
Supreme Court
Court of Appeal
High Court
Crown Court (however, High Court can quash its decisions not related to trial on indictment *R (CPS) v Guildford Crown Court* (2007)

Inferior courts (hear less serious cases) (High Court can quash their decisions)
County Courts
Magistrates' Courts

4.1.3 Civil appellate courts and trial courts

Definition

Trial courts/courts of first instance: The court in which the case is heard for the first time.
Appellate court: A court in which appeals are heard.

Type of court	Type of case heard
Supreme Court	Appellate only
Court of Appeal	Appellate only
High Court Divisional Courts	Appellate only
High Court	First instance and appellate (e.g. in cases which were heard by a Circuit Judge in the County Court fast-track)
County Court	First instance and appellate (post-Woolf Reforms in relation to small claims and fast-track cases)

4.2 Civil Courts of Trial

4.2.1 The High Court

The High Court at first instance		
Queen's Bench	Chancery	Family
Contract and tort	Corporate insolvency Personal insolvency Intellectual property, copyright, patents Trust	Matrimonial cases/ divorce Wardship and adoption cases under the Children Act 1989
		Non-contentious probate, cases under Child Abduction and Custody Act 1985
Three Special Courts: *Commercial Court* Insurance/banking (simpler procedure) *Admiralty Court* Shipping (two lay assessors sit to advise judge) *Technology and Construction Court* (building, engineering, computing)	One Special Court: *Companies Court –* winds up companies	
The biggest division	No juries, cases heard by a single judge	

4.2.2 The County Court

County Court			
Contract	Tort	Claim on the recovery of land	Proceedings under the Children Act 1989
Under £30,000 only for the cases below			
Trusts	Mortgages	Dissolution of partnerships	Contentious probate

4.2.3 The Track System

Once an allocation questionnaire (Form N150) is completed, the allocation judge will assign the case to a track:

£0

£1,000 – limit for personal injury and housing

Small claims track
Usually only one hearing, judge has fl exibility, heard in County Court

---

£5,000

Fast-track
All cases heard in the County Court
Can include simpler cases for a higher amount
Aim: cases heard within 30 weeks, hearing length 1 day, only 1 joint expert witness, no fi xed costs

---

£25,000+

Multi-track
Can include complex cases for a lesser amount
Can be started and heard in either County Court or High Court
Judge can set timetables for pre-trial procedure
Personal injury cases of less than £50,000 must be started in the County Court

---

£50,000

4.2.3.1 Rules relating to transfer between the County Court and the High Court

General issues to be taken into account:

R30.3 Civil Procedure Rules (CPR)
Value of the claim or disputed amount
Convenience/fairness
Availability of specialist judge
Complexity
Public interest
Disability access issues

4.2.3.2 CPR Practice Direction

The cases involving the following issues should not usually be transferred to the County Court:

• Professional negligence

• Fatal accidents

• Allegations of fraud

• Defamation

• Malicious prosecution or false imprisonment

• Claims against the police

• Contentious probate.

4.3 The Civil Justice System: Problems!

Key issues:

**Expense
and
delay**

Leading to

Stress, anxiety, financial hardship for claimants
Pressure to accept low offers
A detrimental impact on evidence available
Unacceptable gaps between compensation and need
Public dissatisfaction

Reforms were suggested in the Heilbron-Hodge Committee (1993) which was built upon by the subsequent Woolf Report.

4.4 The Woolf Report

- Enquiry headed by Lord Justice Woolf
- Interim Report (1995)
- Final Report Access to Justice (1996)
- Recommendations:
  - Creation of the track system

Creation of Civil Procedure Rules to:
create fairness, save money, speed up
the process, ensure proportionality in relation
to cost, importance, complexity and equality
between the parties

See 4.2.3

Specific
rules for case
management and
pre-action protocols

The Woolf Report led to...

The setting of strict
timetables

Both claimant and
defendant can make
offers to settle

Encouragement of Alternative
Dispute Resolution

A penalty for avoiding Alternative Dispute Resolution (ADR) can be incurred but this can be avoided if deemed appropriate on an examination of the relevant factors:

- Nature of dispute
- Merits of the case
- Other attempts to settle
- Cost of mediation
- Delay
- Potential success of mediation.

There is also the possibility to make default and summary judgments.

Definitions

Default judgment: When judgment is given in favour of the claimant as the defendant has not filed the required documents in time.
Summary judgment: Where the defendant has filed the correct documents within the given time but the defence masks the true defence. The court has the power in these circumstances to find for the claimant.

Lord Woolf believed a civil justice system should be…

- **Just** • **Fair** • **Able to offer appropriate procedures**
- **Certain** • **Effective** • **Adequately resourced**
- **Cost effective**   • **Accessible and understandable**
- **Able to give judgments with reasonable speed**

Has this been achieved?

Some research

Goriely *et al.* (2002): The system is now less adversarial, more transparent and there is more willingness to settle. However, in some areas costs rose, cost:damage ratio was the same as pre-Woolf, overall settlement time was the same as pre-Woolf (13 months) but the minimum time was longer due to procedural issues.

Burn (2003): The volume of litigation has fallen **but** the CPR are too lengthy and confusing.

Other issues

Lord Woolf highlighted the need for an efficient IT system but Brooke (2008) states that there is not enough funding in effective IT.

Zander (2009): There is still a delay and the rules appear increasingly more complex, costs have increased.

This led to Lord Justice Jackson's recommendations which will focus on the system of costs and procedural issues.

4.5 Enforcement of Judgment

What happens when one of the parties refuses to pay a court-ordered payment?

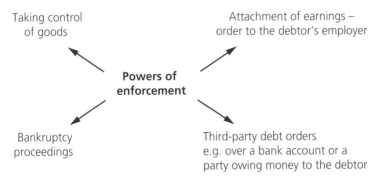

Taking control of goods

Attachment of earnings – order to the debtor's employer

Powers of enforcement

Bankruptcy proceedings

Third-party debt orders e.g. over a bank account or a party owing money to the debtor

However, many judgments still remain unpaid!

4.6 Tribunals

These form a very important part of the legal system.

4.6.1 Administrative tribunals

• Created by statute.

• Ensure that social, welfare, employment and other rights are protected.

• Employment tribunals lie outside of the new unified framework below. There is an Employment Appeal Tribunal from which there can be an appeal to the Court of Appeal.

4.6.2 Tribunals, Courts and Enforcement Act 2007

This builds on the Leggatt Report (2001) and leads to a simplified, unified framework.

4.6.2.1 First-tier tribunal

300,000 cases each year, 200 judges, 3,600 lay members. It includes the following Chambers:

- <u>Social Entitlement</u>
- <u>Health, Education and Social Care</u>
- <u>War Pensions and Armed Forces Compensation</u>
- <u>General</u> *Regulatory*
- *Taxation*
- **Land, Property and Housing**
- Asylum and Immigration

Upper Tribunal
The appellate tribunal

It includes the following Chambers (the cases heard correspond to the formatting of the legal areas):

- <u>Administrative Appeals</u>
- *Tax and Chancery*
- **Lands**
- Asylum and Immigration

The Court of Appeal

Judicial Review
to the Queen's Bench
Administrative Court

4.6.3 Composition and procedure

A tribunal judge sits, sometimes aided by two lay members with relevant and balanced expertise.

4.6.4 The Administrative Justice and Tribunals Council

Established under the Tribunals, Courts and Enforcement Act 2007. It:

- Reviews the work of tribunals.

- Reports on the constitution and working of tribunals.

- Reports on and considers any other relevant matters.

4.6.5 Advantages and disadvantages of tribunals

Advantages	Disadvantages
Cost-effectiveness	
More self-representation	Those who self-represent are more likely to lose the case
	Those who self-represent and win, on average, receive a lower amount
Orders for costs are rarely made	
Speed	
Initially tribunals were quicker than the court system	The volume of work has significantly slowed down the procedure. Greater use of lay members may address this
Simplicity	
Usually more informal and held in private	Those self-representing may find the venue unfamiliar and the procedure confusing due to its unstructured nature
	The role of the judge, particularly in an inquisitorial role, is open to criticism

4.6.6 Domestic tribunals

Definition

Domestic tribunals: 'In-house' tribunals set up by private bodies, e.g. to regulate professions or organisations such as universities. They must follow the rules of natural justice and are open to judicial review.

Research Point

Imagine that you have been dismissed from your work and would like to bring a claim in an employment tribunal. Carry out some research (the Direct.gov website is useful) to determine:

- Whether or not there are any alternatives to making a claim.
- How you would go about submitting a claim.
- The location of your local employment tribunal.

4.7 Alternative Dispute Resolution (ADR)

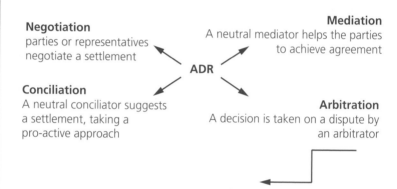

Negotiation
parties or representatives
negotiate a settlement

Mediation
A neutral mediator helps the parties
to achieve agreement

ADR

Conciliation
A neutral conciliator suggests
a settlement, taking a
pro-active approach

Arbitration
A decision is taken on a dispute by
an arbitrator

Voluntary submission
Parties are free to adopt an arbitration agreement
If there is an arbitration agreement in a contract, courts can refuse to hear the dispute
Parties can agree the number of arbitrators (if no agreement, then one)
The form and details of the hearing are determined by the parties
The decision is called an award and is binding on the parties

Advantages of arbitration

- Quality and industry expertise of the arbitrator
- Flexibility to suit parties • Venue and timing can suit parties
- Privacy • Speed • Choice • Cost
- The award is normally final and can be enforced through the courts

Disadvantages of arbitration

- Unexpected, problematic issues of law may arise
- Limited rights of appeal • Professional arbitrators can be expensive
- Formal hearings can be expensive
- There can be delays equal to those in the court system in commercial and international arbitration

In employment cases ADR has been used through the Advisory, Conciliation and Arbitration Services (ACAS). This is quick, informal and private but workers must waive their right to access the Employment Tribunal.

Workpoint

If you were involved in a commercial dispute would you prefer ADR or a court hearing? Give reasons for your answer.

Checkpoint

Task	Done
I understand the difference between civil and criminal law	
I can outline the different types of court in the civil court system	
I can state which type of cases will be heard in which civil courts	
I understand the County Court's Track System and why it is necessary	
I know the recommendations of the Woolf Report	
I can evaluate how the civil court System could be improved	
I can outline the nature of the tribunal system	
I can evaluate the advantages and disadvantages of the tribunal system	
I understand ADR and can evaluate the advantages and disadvantages of arbitration	

Potential exam questions

1) Outline the key differences between how criminal and civil cases are heard.
2) Describe the courts in the civil court system and outline the types of cases they hear.
3) Evaluate how the civil court system could be improved.
4) Describe the tribunal system and analyse its advantages and disadvantages.
5) What forms of ADR are available? Analyse the advantages and disadvantages of ADR.

Chapter 5
Criminal Courts and Procedure

5.1 Introduction

The vast majority of crimes are investigated by the police. This chapter focuses upon the roles of:

- The police
- The Crown Prosecution Service (CPS)
- The criminal courts.

Workpoint

Look back at Chapter 4 and write down the key differences between civil and criminal cases.

5.2 The Criminal Procedure Rules

Definition

The Criminal Procedure Rules: A set of rules, mainly codified in 2005 after the Auld Review, which relate to the practices and procedures in the criminal courts.

5.3 The Crown Prosecution Service

CPS

- Prior to its establishment most prosecutions were carried out by the police
- Set up in 1986
- Governed by the Prosecution of Offences Act 1986
- Headed by the Director of Public Prosecutions
- Aims: make objective assessment of police investigations and prosecute

5.3.1 Code for Crown Prosecutors

Should a prosecution proceed? The Crown Prosecutor follows:

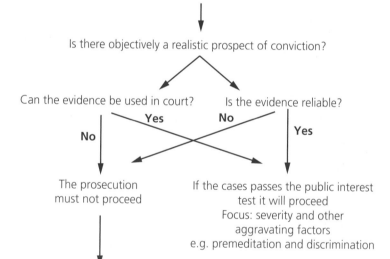

The evidential test

↓

Is there objectively a realistic prospect of conviction?

Can the evidence be used in court?   Is the evidence reliable?

Yes   **No**

No   **Yes**

The prosecution must not proceed

If the cases passes the public interest test it will proceed
Focus: severity and other aggravating factors
e.g. premeditation and discrimination

Following this approach, the amount of discontinued cases **rose**.
Key focus = likelihood of conviction **not** the guilt of the defendant.

5.3.2 The Glidewell Report

Timeline

Pre-1999	Police compiled files and arranged court date **then** sent files to CPS
	CPS **then** made decision whether or not to continue case
1998	The Glidewell Report
	12% of cases discontinued, tensions identified between CPS and police
1999	Recommendation: place CPS representatives into police stations to form an integrated unit
2002–03	CPS Annual Report: increasing number of convictions in cases which proceeded
2003	ss 28–31 Criminal Justice Act 2003: CPS is responsible for determining the charges laid
Ongoing	CPS lawyers in police stations and CPS Direct work in partnership with the police. Discontinuance rates improve but over 1 in 8 cases are discontinued

Workpoint

Describe the development and role of the CPS.

Research Point

Take a look on the CPS website www.cps.gov.uk and discover:

- How you become a CPS lawyer.
- What sort of training is received as a lawyer in the CPS.
- If you would like to be a CPS lawyer.

5.4 Advance Sentence Indication

This is not plea bargaining!

Definition

Plea bargaining: Where the defendant pleads guilty in exchange for a reduction in sentence **or** pleads guilty to a lesser offence on the same facts. This is **not** accepted in English law. It benefits the prosecuting agencies but may:

- Create a feel of injustice for the victim/victim's family
- Lead to over-charging
- Put pressure on the defendant to accept a bargain.

Research Point

In January 2011 Lord Goldsmith called for the use of plea bargaining in the application of the Bribery Act 2010. Carry out research into the use of plea bargaining in the USA and India and determine whether or not you would agree with this and whether or not you think it will ever be introduced.

Definition

Advance Indication of Sentence: Where the defendant instructs counsel to seek an indication from the judge of the maximum sentence which could be imposed if a guilty plea is entered. This is allowed in English law and follows the procedure laid down in *Goodyear* [2005] EWCA Crim 888.

Following on Advance Indication of Sentence:

1. A 'basis of plea' document is submitted. This sets out the facts on which a guilty plea would be entered.

2. The judge may:

3. Following on advance indication of sentence:

Refuse to give an indication

Give an indication which remains binding unless, after time for reasonable consideration, the defendant does not plead guilty.

This procedure is **not** followed in the Magistrates' Court.

5.5 Courts Exercising Criminal Jurisdiction

There is **no** single trial court and **no** single appellate court.

5.6 Appellate Courts

The Court of Justice of the European Communities
References on criminal issues

The Judicial Committee of the Privy Council
Final appeal court for overseas territories, Crown dependencies and Commonwealth countries which retain appeal to the UK court system Leave granted only in exceptional circumstances

Figure continued overleaf

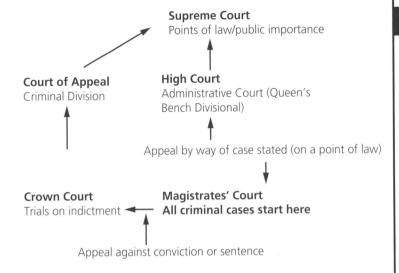

Supreme Court
Points of law/public importance

Court of Appeal
Criminal Division

High Court
Administrative Court (Queen's
Bench Divisional)

Appeal by way of case stated (on a point of law)

Crown Court
Trials on indictment

Magistrates' Court
All criminal cases start here

Appeal against conviction or sentence

5.7 Criminal Courts of First Instance

The Crown Court: Key facts
It is referred to as a single court
Juries are used as part of the trial process
Can sentence persons convicted in the Magistrates' Court
Jury determines issues of fact, judges decide questions of law
High Court, Circuit Judges, Recorders, District Judges and Justices of the Peace can sit
The Crown Court in London is the Central Criminal Court, also known as the Old Bailey

The Magistrates' Court: Key facts
Has some civil jurisdiction but deals with **98%** of all criminal matters
Jurisdiction:
• Summary offences
• Either way offences
• Preliminary matters in indictable only offences

There are two types of magistrate:

Lay magistrates	Stipendiary magistrates
Also known as Justices of the Peace	Now known as District Judges
Generally not legally qualified	Will have been solicitors or barristers for at least seven years
Unpaid	Salaried
Volunteers from the local area	
Have some training	
Supported by a qualified court clerk	
Part-time	Full-time
Approx. 30,000 deputies	Approx. 100 plus deputies

5.8 Classification of criminal offences

Magistrates' Court
All criminal offences start here
2% go up to the Crown Court
No committals of indictable offences
but deal with legal aid, bail and remand
Limited sentencing:

- 6 months imprisonment
- £1,000 fine
- Or a statutory fine up to £5,000

Crown Court
Trial by jury

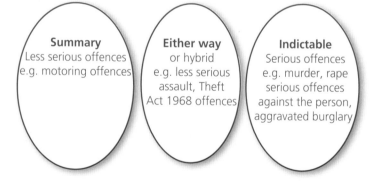

Summary
Less serious offences
e.g. motoring offences

Either way
or hybrid
e.g. less serious
assault, Theft
Act 1968 offences

Indictable
Serious offences
e.g. murder, rape
serious offences
against the person,
aggravated burglary

Offences triable either way. Some issues:

- These offences have no automatic 'home' in either court.
- To find these types of offences a 'home':

First: A plea before venue is made at the Magistrates' Court. Defendant can request an indication of sentence which is given at the Magistrates' discretion. If an indication is given and the defendant chooses to plead **not guilty**, then the indication is not binding

Guilty – Magistrates pass sentence   **Not guilty**

Mode of trial or 'allocation' hearing
Under s 19 Magistrates' Court Act 1980 the Court is informed about previous convictions to assess whether sentencing powers are adequate Allocation guidelines aid the magistrates, these include an examination of the nature of the case and the powers of the court

Suitable for summary hearing
Defendant can choose if they wish to be tried on indictment or not

Not suitable for summary hearing
Sent to Crown Court for hearing on indictment

If a summary trial is chosen then the sentence cannot exceed magistrates' sentencing powers

What factors can influence the defendant's choice of court?

The Crown Court

Advantages
On a **not guilty** plea, conviction rate is **lower**
Difficult to gain leave to appeal

Disadvantages
Delay, however, during this delay the CPS may choose not to proceed
Difficult to gain leave to appeal. However, leave may be granted if the jury are not properly directed

The Magistrates' Court

Advantages
Maximum sentence is **lower**
Less publicity/interest
No leave required to appeal to the Crown Court
Reasons required therefore easier to discover error

Disadvantages
On a **not guilty** plea, conviction rate is **higher**

Workpoint

Determine whether you would advise a client charged with theft to choose a summary trial or a trial on indictment, and give your reasoning.

5.9 The 'Right' to Trial by Jury

Where the defendant has a choice (check above in which cases this would be relevant), there have been proposals to restrict the defendant's choice of a jury trial. This has **not** become law.

The restriction of choice was recommended in the Auld Report 2001 **but has still not become law.**

The Auld Report did, however lead to:

The Criminal Justice Act 2003
Key sections outlining trial without jury

Section 43
In serious or complex fraud cases
If the trial is burdensome as to prejudice the interests of justice

Section 44
Where there is a substantial risk of jury tampering

Checkpoint

Task	Done
I can outline the nature and role of the CPS	
I know how the CPS decides whether a case should proceed	
I know the history of how the CPS developed to prosecute the majority of crimes	
I understand the nature of the criminal court system and the role of each court	
I know the system of appeals in the criminal court system	
I can define the terms summary, either way and indictable and I know which courts hear which type of case	

Checkpoint (continued)

Task	Done
I understand the approach taken in relation to where offences triable either way will be heard	
I understand the advantages and disadvantages of both summary trials and trials on indictment	
I know the circumstances in which trial by jury can be denied	

Potential exam questions

1) Describe how the Crown Prosecution Service functions.
2) Evaluate criticisms of the Crown Prosecution Service and the extent to which these have been addressed.
3) Define the Magistrates' Court and Crown Court and analyse the relationship between the two.
4) To what extent do you believe that a defendant should have a choice in mode of trial in relation to triable either way offences?

Chapter 6

Appeals

Lord Woolf: Access to Justice (1996)
The aims of the appeals system

Private: Justice for individuals

Public: Supporting public confidence
Clarifying/developing the law

6.1 Appeals in Civil Proceedings

Workpoint

Before studying this area, draw a simple diagram of the court system as studied in Chapter 2.

Access to Justice Act 1999
(provides a framework alongside the Civil Procedure Rules)

- In a civil case the right to an appeal is **not** automatic.

- *Tanfern Ltd v Gregor Cameron-MacDonald* (2000)
  In civil cases, the appeal is generally to the next **judge** not **court** (this is different from criminal cases – see below) For second-tier (second) appeals, the point of principle or practice must be an important one.

Court	Appeals heard
High Court	Hears appeals in the Divisional Court
Court of Appeal (Civil Division)	Hears civil appeals from the multi track
Supreme Court	Hears appeals in civil cases from England, Northern Ireland and Scotland
Privy Council	Civil appeals from the Commonwealth Hears devolution issues

Remember: The European Court of Justice (ECJ) does **not** hear appeals but answers references on questions of European Union law. See 1.8.

Leave to appeal is nearly always needed.

The Appeal Court will **review** the decision of the lower court and grant leave if:

The decision of the lower court is **wrong**	The decision was unjust due to serious procedural or other irregularity.

The Appeal Court has all the power of the lower court and can.

- Affirm
- Set aside
- Vary the lower court's order or judgment
- Refer a claim for determination by the lower court
- Order a new trial
- Make a costs order.

Definition

Senior Courts of England and Wales: The High Court, the Crown Court and the Court of Appeal.

The key courts

*Established by Judicature Act 1873
*There are 37 Lords Justices of Appeal plus:

- Lord Chief Justice
- President of the Family Division of the High Court
- Vice-Chancellor of the Chancery Division of the High Court
- Master of the Rolls.

Court of Appeal
(Civil Division)

*High Court judges may sit

*There are usually four or five courts each day

*Twelve Justices of the Supreme Court sit

*Judges sit in threes but can sit in fives for important cases

*Created in October 2009 to replace the Appellate Committee of the House of Lords.

The Supreme Court

*Hears appeals from:

*In general, hears appeals of general public importance

- High Court – leapfrog (see below)
- Court of Appeal Civil Division (with permission from CA or SC)
- Courts in Northern Ireland and Scotland.

Definition

Leapfrog appeal: A **civil** appeal from the High Court can bypass the Court of Appeal and go straight to the Supreme Court, e.g.

Supreme Court

Court of Appeal (Civil)   Leapfrog

High Court

This can happen if the trial judge finds:

- A point of law of general public importance is involved.

- The point of law is one in which the judge is bound following the doctrine of *stare decisis*.

- The Supreme Court gives leave (permission) to appeal.

Workpoint

Close the book and sketch a drawing of the appeals in the civil court system.

Research Point

Find three examples of leapfrog appeals in the Law Reports (one is *Anderton v Ryan* [1985] AC 560). See if you can find any similarities in these cases. To what extent do you think that the leapfrog appeal is important in order to ensure the development of the law?

The Privy Council
No longer hears devolution issues (the Supreme Court now does)
Hears mainly civil cases
Hears appeals from outside the UK
Is the final appeal court of Channel Islands and Isle of Man
Can hear appeals from: • Prize courts   • Ecclesiastical courts   • Medical tribunals
Can hear special cases referred by the Crown

Research Point

Access the website of the Judicial Committee of the Privy Council at www.jcpc.gov.uk and find out more about:

• its role

• its powers

• the amount and kinds of cases it hears each year.

6.2 Appeals in Criminal Proceedings

Court	Appeals heard
Crown Court	Hears appeals on fact and sentencing from the Magistrates' Court

continued overleaf

Court	Appeals heard
High Court	Appeals by way of case stated heard at the Administrative Court (Queen's Bench Divisional)
Court of Appeal	Criminal Division hears appeals from the Crown Court
Supreme Court	Hears appeals from English courts and Northern Ireland
Privy Court	Appeals from the Commonwealth where special leave has been granted. There needs to be exceptional circumstances or a substantial injustice and the denial of a fair trial

Remember: The ECJ does **not** hear appeals but answers references on questions of European Union law. See 1.8.

6.3 Prosecution Appeals

s 36 Criminal Justice Act 1972
After an acquittal the prosecution can refer a point of law to the Court of Appeal This does not affect the original defendant who has the right to present argument

s 36 Criminal Justice Act 1988
After a conviction and sentence in the Crown Court, the Attorney General can refer an 'unduly lenient sentence' to the Court of Appeal which has the power to increase it

ss 54 and 55 Criminal Procedure and Investigations Act 1996
Power for the prosecution to appeal against a jury acquittal in the case of jury intimidation

Figure continued overleaf

The Criminal Justice Act 2003
Result of the Auld Report 2001

ss 57–63
Prosecution and defence can appeal against a trial
judge's error in law which terminates a case before
the jury returns a verdict

ss 75 and 76
Abolish double jeopardy
Now a re-trial can take place if there is:
new and **compelling** evidence of guilt and it is in the public interest
The rules are retrospective
There are 30 'qualifying offences'

6.4 Defence Appeals

The mode of appeal is **always** governed by the place of the original trial.

High Court
Administrative Court (Queen's Bench Divisional)
Both prosecution and defence can appeal but **only** on the grounds that:

- The Magistrates' decision was wrong in law; or
- The Magistrates exceeded their jurisdiction.

This is known as 'by way of case stated'. Court works from written
documents. Appeal is possible to the Supreme Court if a point of law of
general public importance is involved and leave is obtained from either
court.

Crown Court
Appeals available on **fact** or **law** or both
Only available for the **defence**

Initial plea:

• Not guilty: appeal allowed against sentence, conviction or both
• Guilty: **only** allowed appeal against sentence

Appeal: Full hearing, sentence cannot exceed powers of Magistrates

Magistrates' Court Summary trial

Workpoint

Outline the differences between the powers of the prosecution and
defence to appeal the decision of a lower court.

Supreme Court

Criminal Appeal Act 1968 s33 governs leave to appeal to the Supreme Court: the Court of Appeal must certify:

- The case involves a point of law of general public importance (for criminal cases only).
- This point is one which should be considered by the Supreme Court.

Court of Appeal

Criminal Appeal Act 1968:

Appeal should only be allowed against conviction if it is felt that the conviction is **unsafe**.

s 4: The court has discretion to hear new evidence

Crown Court Trial on indictment

6.5 The Criminal Cases Review Commission

The Criminal Cases Review Commission (CCRC)
Established by ss 8–12 of the Criminal Appeal Act 1995
It is an independent body
It is **not** a court
Refers cases: - Crown Court to Court of Appeal - Magistrates' Court to the Crown Court
Role: - Review/investigate cases of suspected wrongful conviction/ sentence - Refer to appropriate court when there is a real possibility of conviction/verdict/finding or sentence not being upheld – established through new legal argument or information
Normal rights of appeal should be exhausted prior to review
196 cases were referred in first six years

Workpoint

How effective do you believe the Criminal Cases Review Commission is in ensuring that justice is achieved?

Research Point

Access the Criminal Cases Review Commission page on the www. justice.gov.uk website. How does an individual submit an application to the Commission? How is this application then dealt with?

Checkpoint

Task	Done
I know how the civil appeals system functions	
I understand the technicalities of granting leave to appeal in civil cases	
I know which courts hear appeals in the civil court system	
I know how the criminal appeals system functions	
I understand the technicalities of granting leave to appeal in criminal cases	
I know which courts hear appeals in the criminal court system	
I understand the changes introduced by the Criminal Justice Act 2003	
I understand the role and powers of the Criminal Cases Review Commission	

Potential exam questions

1) Explain why appeals are needed.
2) Outline the system of civil appeal courts and how leave to appeal is granted.
3) Outline the system of criminal appeal courts and how leave to appeal is granted.
4) Explain and evaluate the impact of the Criminal Justice Act 2003 on the criminal appeals system.

Chapter 7
Funding

7.1 Access to Justice

I need advice on a legal issue

- I don't know any law
- How much money is needed? (around £100/£600 per hour)
- Where is the nearest solicitor?
- How do I talk to a lawyer? They scare me!
- If I can't get help, will I be denied access to justice?

Some routes for advice:

- Citizens' Advice Bureaux – www.citizensadvice.org.uk

- The Legal Services Commission – www.legalservices.gov.uk/default.asp

A very important issue in relation to access to justice is **the cost**.

Ask three people you know who have not studied the legal system how they would go about:

- Making a claim against builders who did a 'botched' job.

- Bringing a complaint against the police.

- Claiming against an online seller who has not delivered paid-for goods.

Did you find any key themes? Did your respondents know how to access legal advice? Did any of them state that they would not pursue the issue due to time and/or cost? Can you make any conclusions on how accessible the legal system is?

7.2 Public Funding

Timeline

1903 Poor Prisoners' Defence Act
1930 Poor Prisoners' Defence Act
These provided limited representation in criminal cases

1945 Rushcliffe Committee Report, key recommendations:
- Legal aid should be available in all courts
- The availability of legal aid should not be limited
- Legal aid should be means-tested
- The State should bear the cost
- Legal aid lawyers should receive 'adequate' pay

1949 Legal Aid and Advice Act
- Law Society given duty of ensuring legal aid and advice are available
- This scheme initially only covered civil cases

1964 The legal aid scheme was extended to criminal cases

1978 48% qualified for legal aid

1979 Limits increased so more than 80% qualified for legal aid

1984 Police and Criminal Evidence Act creates duty solicitor schemes in police stations

1988 Legal Aid Act consolidates the system and the handling of civil legal aid was given to the Legal Aid Board

1990 Around 48% eligible for legal aid

1999 Access to Justice Act: the number eligible continues to fall, only the poorest are now eligible

Figure continued overleaf

Civil matters
- Direct money where most needed
- Ensure fairness
- Provide value for money
- Have a controlled, affordable budget

White Paper: Modernising Justice Cm4155 1998

Recommendations

Criminal matters
- Balance: protection of defendants versus value for money
- Fairness needed
- Impartial defence needed
- Confidence in the system needed
- PACE s 58(1) enshrines right to consult a solicitor
- ECHR Art 6(3) includes right to legal assistance

This White Paper led to:

The Access to Justice Act 1999

- Establishes the Legal Services Commission with two services:
- **Civil**: Community Legal Service
- **Criminal**: Criminal Defence Service
- Government-funded with an annual fixed amount
- Criminal cases can be funded from any civil case surplus
- s 8: Criteria for funding civil cases
- Schedule 3: Criteria for right to representation in criminal cases
- s 13(2) The Commission is given the power to employ
  lawyers. This led to the Public Defender Service

7.3 The Legal Services Commission

Contracts with solicitors' firms and not-for-profit agencies

The number of solicitors with
contracts to undertake publicly
funded work in civil cases has
fallen drastically

Pre-1999 = Approx. 10,000 firms

2007–8 = 2,230 firms

These firms need to gain
a quality mark

7.4 Public Funding in Civil Matters

7.4.1 Limitations on funding

Level	Covers	Does not cover
Legal help	Advice	Issuing/conducting court proceedings
Help at court	Advice and advocacy at court	Formal legal representation
Legal representation	All aspects of the case	
Support funding	Partial funding in cases being pursued privately	
Approved family help	Advice, negotiation, issuing of proceedings, required conveyancing	
Family mediation	Cost of mediation to resolve a family dispute	

7.4.2 Criteria

Section 8 Access to Justice Act 1999:

- Cost
- Benefit
- Availability of funds
- Importance to the individual
- Availability of other (non-funded) services
- Prospects of success
- Conduct of the individual
- Public interest
- Other factors as the Lord Chancellor may order to be considered.

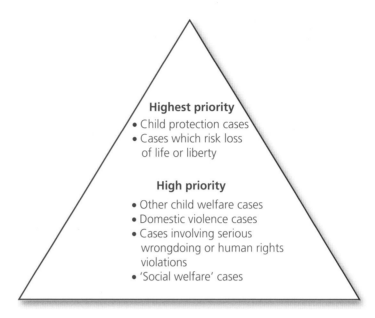

Highest priority
- Child protection cases
- Cases which risk loss of life or liberty

High priority
- Other child welfare cases
- Domestic violence cases
- Cases involving serious wrongdoing or human rights violations
- 'Social welfare' cases

However, in relation to 'social welfare' matters, generally only advice is covered. Help will only be given where there is sufficient benefit to the client.

7.4.3 Reasons to refuse funding

If other avenues (e.g. Ombudsman) should be and have not been pursued.

Full representation will be refused if a conditional fee agreement is likely to be available.

Full representation will also be refused if prospects of success are:

Unclear   Borderline without any wider public interest   Poor

---

Access to Justice Act 1999 Schedule 2:
Matters excluded from funding

- Allegations of negligence (not clinical)
- Conveyancing
- Boundary disputes
- Making a will
- Trusts
- Defamation/Malicious falsehood
- Company/partnership law
- Other business matters
- Matters not relating to the law of England and Wales

The merits test in relation to the
granting of funding requires

A prospect of success   A finding that it is reasonable
to fund the case

Following this, Full Representation will be refused unless:

	Moderate	Good	Very good
Prospects of success are:	50%	60%	80%
Ratio of damages to costs needs to be:	4:1	2:1	Damages will exceed costs

Some criticisms of Civil Legal Aid

- In some areas there are no Legal Aid-funded advice providers. This could lead to higher fees
- Sometimes clients are not referred to appropriate advice providers
- Some advice can be poor or even damaging
- **[ECtHR]** *Steel and Morris v UK (App No 6841/01):* Denial of Legal Aid in defamation cases infringes Art 6 of the ECHR

Legal Aid reform

In June 2011 the Government introduced the Legal Aid, Sentencing and Punishment of Offenders Bill for its first reading in the House of Commons. This Bill outlines plans to cut Legal Aid from areas such as employment, immigration, debt and medical negligence. If these proposals become law they will have a significant impact on access to civil Legal Aid.

7.5 The Criminal Defence Service

The right to legal representation is a basic human right enshrined in Article 6 ECHR.

Therefore, the Criminal Defence Service created under s 12 of the Access to Justice Act 1999 and established in April 2001 covers:

Duty solicitor schemes   Advice/Assistance   Representation

Duty solicitors

• Since May 2004, not available (unless client is vulnerable) in cases of:

  • Non-imprisonable offences
  • Drink/drive offences
  • Arrest on a warrant
  • Breach of bail

• Relevant law: s 13 Access to Justice Act 1999

• Requests routed through Criminal Defence Direct telephone service

Advice and assistance

- Limited to one hour
- Means-tested (although duty solicitor can see all under the Advice and Assistance scheme free of charge)
- Not available when:
  - Offender is on bail charged with a non-imprisonable offence
  - Trial is in the Magistrates' court

Representation covers:

Cost of solicitor preparing case	Cost of representation in court	Cost of barrister if required

Test = based on merits (this test is waived for Crown Court cases)

Schedule 3 Access to Justice Act 1999, key factors:

1. The likelihood of loss of liberty or serious damage to reputation.
2. Whether a substantial point of law will arise.
3. The capacity of the individual to understand the case.
4. The likelihood of the need for tracing, interviewing or expert cross-examination.
5. If it is in the interests of another person that the individual is represented.

The Public Defender Service
- Established under the Access to Justice Act 1999
- First five set up in 2001(plus one in 2002 and two in 2003)
- Controversy: the State both prosecutes and defends

Positive:
- Lawyers more likely to attend police stations, leading to less likelihood of a charge being made

Negative:
- Clients more likely to plead guilty with no advantage
- Not as cost-effective as private firms, four offices therefore closed down in 2007

> **Research Point**
>
> Analyse why it is a human right that representation is available in criminal cases. To what extent do you believe that the current system achieves justice?

7.6 The Legal Profession and Public Funding

The number of legal aid solicitors has decreased (in 2011 only 6% of lawyers undertook legal aid work). The key reason: lawyers are unhappy about changes to legal aid contracts.

R (Law Society) v Legal Services Commission and *Dexter Montague (A firm) v Legal Services Commission* [2007] EWCA Civ 1264:

- A challenge was successful in relation to the changes to contracts for legal aid work.

- Almost unlimited power of amendment to the contract was not sufficiently transparent.

7.6.1 Reform

7.6.1.1 The Carter Report: Legal Aid – A Market-Based Approach To Reform July 2006

Key recommendations:

- 'Best value' tendering
- Fixed fees for solicitors working in police stations
- Revise graduated fees for Crown Court advocates
- Graduated fee scheme for Crown Court litigators.

This could lead to fewer firms providing legal aid services and the increased potential for 'advice deserts'.

7.7 Private Funding

Paying for legal advice and representation can be:

Costly   and   Unpredictable

This led to the introduction of **Conditional Fee Agreements (CFAs)**.

Conditional Fee Agreements: An agreement made by the lawyer and client that a success fee will be paid to the lawyer if the case is won. The lawyer does not gain a share of any damages awarded.

Key facts: Conditional fee arrangements
Created by s 58 Courts and Legal Services Act 1990
Implemented in 1995 by Conditional Fee Agreements Regulations 1995 (SI 1995 No 1674)
Can be used in all civil claims including a money claim (and since the Access to Justice Act 1999, civil claims which do not include a money claim)
Agreement is reached by lawyer and client (issue: the success fee could potentially absorb all the client's damages)
Access to Justice Act 1999: Success fee can be claimed as costs of the case
June 2004 rules on road accident cases: Losing party will pay a 12.5% success fee on out-of-court settlements and 100% if the case goes to trial
Some claims firms which relied on CFAs went into liquidation despite initial success

After-the-event insurance is also available.

Definition

After-the-event insurance: Insurance which allows claimants to insure against the risk of paying costs after a claim has begun. The premium has to be paid before the case begins. After s 29 Access to Justice Act 1999 the premium can now be claimed as part of court costs.

7.8 Advice Agencies

Key issue: Lack of co-ordination

Therefore, Community Legal Service Partnerships were created (see 7.2 above).

However:

• Sometimes these agencies find themselves in direct competition

• These agencies are encouraged to gain a Quality Mark (see 7.3 above), this can be time-consuming.

Citizens' Advice Bureaux

• Set up in 1938
• Around 2,000 offices
• General advice on social welfare, debt and also legal advice
• Increased caseload due to legal aid shrinkage
• Experiencing difficulty in finding appropriate lawyers for clients

---

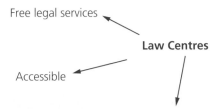

Free legal services

Law Centres

Accessible

Focus on areas with a lack of solicitors

Definition

Pro-bono work: 'for the public good'. Advice for those who cannot afford to pay, given for example by the Free Representation Unit (FRU). Many law schools have successful, supported *pro-bono* schemes.

Workpoint

Analyse the extent to which you believe that advice agencies can help individuals access justice.

Checkpoint

Task	Done
I know how funding and knowledge impact access to justice	
I understand how the legal aid system developed	
I understand the impact of the Access to Justice Act 1999	
I know the role of the Legal Services Commission and the services it provides	
I know which types of civil cases will be eligible for legal aid	
I know how the Criminal Defence Service functions	
I know key issues relating to private funding of legal cases	
I know how other agencies can aid people to access justice	

Potential exam questions

1) Outline how issues of funding impact on access to justice and, in the light of this, describe the development of the legal aid system.
2) Evaluate the changes to the legal aid system introduced by the Access to Justice Act 1999.
3) Outline which types of civil case are eligible for legal aid.
4) Describe how the Criminal Defence Service functions and evaluate to what extent it serves to achieve justice.
5) Critically analyse the impact of recent reforms to the legal aid system.

Chapter 8

Juries

8.1 Juries: Timeline

Pre-1215 Some evidence that juries were used

1215 The Magna Carta recognises right to trial by judgment of peers. Juries become usual method for the trying of criminal cases

The role of juries develops with a focus on local knowledge rather than decision-making

Late 1400s Role of juries becomes akin to independent assessors and deciders of fact

1670 *Bushell's Case* (1670) Vaughan 135: Juries are the sole arbiters of fact, a judge cannot challenge their decision

1960 [CA] *R v McKenna* [1960] 2 All ER 326: Judges cannot put undue pressure on a jury

Court	Crown Court	High Court Queen's Bench Division	County Court	Coroner's Court
Number of jurors	12	12	8	7–11
When used	In all trials	Rarely. In cases of defamation, false imprisonment and malicious prosecution	Very rarely used. In cases of defamation, false imprisonment and malicious prosecution	In certain cases in which deaths occur in custody, where police officers are involved or which occurred in certain accidents
Role	Decide guilt	Decide liability and amount of damages	Decide liability and amount of damages	To determine the cause of death

8.2 Jury Qualifications

Be aged between 18 and 70

Be an elector

**s 1 Juries Act 1974
A juror must...**

Have lived in the UK for at least five years

Not be 'mentally disordered'
This leads to disqualification under Schedule 1 Criminal Justice Act 2003

Definition

Mentally disordered

- Resident in a mental health institution
- Regularly treated for a mental health issue
- Under guardianship under section 7 of the Mental Health Act 1983
- Has been judged incapable of administering his or her affairs

---

Disqualification

Permanent

Those sentenced to:

- Life imprisonment
- Detention during Her Majesty's or the Secretary of State's pleasure
- Imprisonment for the protection of the public
- An extended sentence
- A term of imprisonment or detention of five years or more.

Disqualification (continued)

For 10 years

Those who have:

- Served a term of imprisonment in the previous five years
- Had a suspended sentence passed on them
- Had a community order or other community sentence passed on them.

For a varying term

- Those currently on bail cannot sit as a juror and can be fined if they do not declare this.

Excusal

- Pre-April 2004 judges, lawyers and police were not eligible. The Criminal Justice Act 2003 abolished this category.
- Since April 2004 judges can serve but should do so as a private citizen, declare any links to court staff and follow the directions of the trial judge.
- Pre-April 2004 essential occupations such as healthcare staff could be excused, now they can only be granted discretionary excusal if there is very good reason. Reasons include:
  - Illness
  - Disability access issues
  - Being a mother of a small baby
  - Examinations
  - Urgent business commitments.
- Members of the armed forces can be excused.
- The eligibility of police and lawyers has been questioned as a potential breach of Article 6 ECHR following:
  - *R v Abdroikof* [2007] UKHL 37
  - *R v Green* [2007] UKHL 37
  - *R v Williamson* [2007] UKHL 37.

The key issue is whether or not there is the potential for bias. If there is, a conviction can be quashed or a re-trial ordered.

See also C. Thomas, *Diversity and Fairness in the Jury System* (2007) Ministry of Justice Research Series. The key findings were:

- Juries are representative in gender, age and race.

- The only under-represented groups were those in lower socio-economic groups and unemployed people.

Who can sit as a juror and who cannot? Have you ever sat as a juror? If yes, review your experience in the light of your study of the law. Did you believe it achieved justice? If no, would you like to sit as a juror? Would you think that your input would lead to justice being achieved?

8.3 Selection at Court

8.3.1 Jurors

Jurors:

- Are selected randomly by computer from the electoral register.
- Are usually in service for two weeks. If the case will be much longer, warning is given.
- Can be discharged if he or she cannot understand English.
- Can be discharged due to disability under s 9B(2) of the Juries Act 1974. For example, blind people may not be able to see photographs and deaf people may need a signer and there cannot be an extra person in the jury room.
- Are given an information leaflet pre-trial.
- Are encouraged to report any concerns about the behaviour and attitude of other jurors.

8.3.1.1 Vetting

In criminal cases the prosecution and defence can see the list of potential jurors.

There are two types of vetting

Where routine police checks eliminate those who are disqualified:	Check on background and political convictions:
R v Mason (1980) 3 All ER 777 Held: this form of vetting was merely reventing the crime of acting as a juror while disqualified	Practice Note (Jury: Stand By: Jury Checks) (1988) 3 All ER 1086: This should only be used with the AG's permission in exceptional cases which involve: • National security with evidence given in secret • Terrorist cases

Figure continued overleaf

15 jurors are initially put into a group

↓

Of these, the court clerk chooses 12 at random

↓

The prosecution and defence can then challenge in two main ways

To the array	For cause
s 5 Juries Act 1974 Challenge on the basis that the jury is unrepresentative or biased	Challenges the right of an individual juror to sit if, for example, they are disqualified or related to the defendant

Definition

Right to stand by jurors: The prosecution's right, after the vetting procedure, to put a juror at the end of the list of potential jurors so it is unlikely that they will be used. No reasons need to be given but this should be used rarely.

Workpoint

Explain the process by which a jury is selected at court. Can anyone be excluded from a jury?

8.4 Juries in Civil Cases

Remember that juries in civil cases not only decide who wins but also set the level of damages.

Use of juries in Civil Cases

- 1971 Faulks Committee report recommended the abolition of juries in defamation cases due to technicalities, complexity and expense.
- However, they are retained and managed under s 66 County Courts Act 1984 and s 69 Senior Courts Act 1981.
- s 69 Senior Courts Act 1981 states that jury trials can be allowed when it involves:
  - A charge of fraud
  - A claim in respect of libel, slander, malicious prosecution or false imprisonment.

Unless the case would involve a prolonged investigation of evidence which could not be made 'conveniently' by a jury.

Figure continued overleaf

Defamation cases

- 'Conveniently' was taken in *Goldsmith v Pressdram Ltd* (1987) as relating to the achievement of justice. However, in the case *McDonald's Corporation v Steel and Morris* (1997), a jury trial was denied due to the potential length of the case.
- *Beta Construction Ltd v Channel Four TV Co Ltd* (1990) lays down some considerations in the determination of whether a jury trial should be allowed. These include:
  - How much the jury's presence will affect the length of the trial
  - Any practical difficulties relating to evidence
  - Any special complexities or technicalities.
- After some very large awards of damages made by juries, the Court of Appeal under the Courts and Legal Services Act 1990 can now, and often does, reduce the awards made.

Malicious prosecutions

- Presumption in favour of jury trial but no automatic right
- As with defamation cases, if the circumstances in s 69(3) Senior Courts Act 1981 arise, then jury trial can be denied

Juries in Personal Injury Cases

- Applications are very rare
- *Ward v James* (1965) 1 All ER 563 Guidelines:
  - Personal injury cases should normally be tried by a single judge applying conventional scales of damages
  - Jury trials should only be allowed in exceptional circumstances (an example could be where injuries resulted from a deliberate misuse of power)
- Since *Ward v James* there has only been one other jury trial on a personal injury case

Workpoint

To what extent do you think that it is necessary to have jury trials in civil cases?

8.5 Juries in Coroners' Courts

Key issues

- Use of a jury is discretionary unless a death occurs:

    1. In prison
    2. In an industrial accident
    3. In circumstances concerning the public's health and safety
    4. In police custody

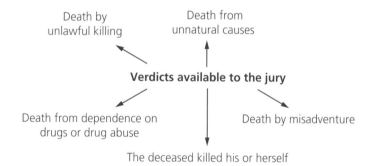

S7 Coroners and Justice Act 2009
(not yet in force):
Jury will only be used if a death occurs in police custody if:
- The death was violent or unnatural or the cause is unknown
- The death resulted from the act or omission of a police officer
- The death was caused by a notable accident, poisoning or disease

Death by unlawful killing   Death from unnatural causes

Verdicts available to the jury

Death from dependence on drugs or drug abuse   Death by misadventure

The deceased killed his or herself

8.6 Juries in Criminal Cases

Workpoint

Before you look at this area, turn back to Chapter 5 and revise your understanding of the criminal court system.

This is the most important use of juries (in around 1% of all criminal cases).

Juries are used in Crown Court to determine guilt and points of fact in:

Offences tried on indictment

Offences triable either way (about 1 in every 20 defendants choose to go to the Crown Court)

Definition

Directed acquittal: When the judge at the end of the prosecution case directs the jury to acquit as he or she decides that in law the prosecution's evidence has not made out a case against the defendant. This happens in about 10% of cases.

Trial without jury

• s 44 Criminal Justice Act 2003
Allowed if there is '*a real and present danger that jury tampering would take place*'
e.g. *R v Twomey and others* (2009)

• Domestic Violence, Crime and Victims Act 2004
Allowed where jury has convicted defendant of some offences but there a still a large number of related counts to be decided

8.6.1 Verdicts

• A judge sums up a case to the jury and directs them on any law; *Bushell's Case*(1670): a judge must accept the jury's verdict
• The jury deliberates in a private room and should first:

  • Come to a unanimous decision
  • If not, after two hours the judge can direct that a majority verdict is acceptable (this occurs in around one fifth of convictions)

    This can be 10:2 or 11:1

• If jury (through e.g. illness falls below 12) the verdict can be:

    10:1 or 9:1

• If there are only 9 jurors then ALL must agree

• s 17(3) Juries Act 1974: If a majority decision to convict is returned the foreperson MUST announce the number of both those against and those for.

8.7 Secrecy of the Jury Room

8.7.1 Contempt of Court Act 1981 s 8

Disclosure of what happens in the jury room is contempt of court, a criminal offence.

Key issue

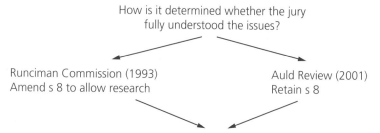

How is it determined whether the jury fully understood the issues?

Runciman Commission (1993)
Amend s 8 to allow research

Auld Review (2001)
Retain s 8

Jury Research and Impropriety CP04/05 (2005)
- Majority were in favour of some level of research but against allowing an independent party access to the jury room
- The use of CCTV in the jury room was rejected by most

However, s 8 has not been amended

Workpoint

To what extent do you believe that s 8 of the Contempt of Court Act 1981 should be amended to allow research into juries? Write a sample essay plan to set out how you would answer this question.

8.7.2 The Common Law Rule

Case:	
***Vaise v Delaval* (1785)**	Court refused to consider sworn statements from two jurors relating to how they made a decision
***R v Thompson* (1962)**	Even where a foreman produced a list of the defendant's past convictions the court would not accept evidence of what happened in the jury room

However, this does not apply outside of the jury room.

Case:	
R v Young (1995)	A conviction was quashed after it was discovered that the jury held a séance overnight to contact the victim

Does this infringe upon Art 6 ECHR Right to a Fair Trial?

Case:	
R v Connor: R v Mizra (Conjoined Appeals) (2004)	Answer: no, by majority verdict as: • Confidentiality is essential • There was a need for finality • Jurors need to be protected from harassment

However, Lord Steyn dissented stating there could be a breach if a real risk of racial bias found.

Case:	
Practice Direction (Crown Court: Guidance to Jurors) (2004)	A juror can bring any concerns about fellow jurors to the trial judge

Workpoint

Consider the case of *R v Young* (1995) above. If the séance had taken place in the jury room then the court would have no power to dismiss the jury. In the light of this, analyse whether or not you believe the strict distinction between the jury room and the jury's actions outside the room should be upheld.

8.8 Research into Juries

Key issue: What happens in the jury room is **secret**.

Definition

Shadow jury: A jury which sits in a courtroom and withdraws at the same time as the actual jury but its deliberations take place in front of cameras. *The Shadow Jury at Work* (1974) found that shadow juries take their work very seriously.

Mock jury: A jury which watches or listens to a simulated case and then deliberates in front of cameras.

8.8.1 Other research

Baldwin and McConville *Jury Trials* (1979):

- Compared attitudes of lawyers and judges with 500 jury verdicts.

- Found one out of four acquittals and one out of twenty convictions found to be doubtful or highly questionable by three or more respondents. In relation to convictions, black defendants were more likely to fall into this category.

Zander and Henderson *Royal Commission on Criminal Justice* (1993):

- Questionnaire-based research.

- Over 90% of jurors stated that the jury as a whole had understood the evidence **but** under 10% of jurors admitted they had some difficulty.

- Lawyers and judges stated that 2–4% of verdicts were surprising and inexplicable; the police thought 8% were.

> **Research Point**
>
> Locate two recent research reports on the use of juries, such as Professor Cheryl Thomas' 2010 study *Are Juries Fair?*. Try to find one relating to the UK and one to another jurisdiction. Can you see any key trends over the years? How does the experience in another jurisdiction relate to that of the UK?

8.8.2 Jury trials

Advantages	Disadvantages
Public confidence	Racial bias and composition
• The public believe in the impartiality and fairness of trial by peers • It is seen as more open and that it encourages transparency • Prevents professional dominance in the criminal justice system	• Baldwin and McConville (1979) found that black defendants' convictions were more likely to be seen as doubtful • Cheryl Thomas (2007): No significant finding of any bias • Recommendations to reform the system to change the balance have been rejected due to issues relating to true representation and the relationships between the jurors

Advantages	Disadvantages
Jury equity • Juries are not bound to follow binding legal authority • Juries do not have to give reasons • They are seen to be more likely to focus on 'fairness'	**Media influence** • In high-profile cases the media may influence judges • This could lead to convictions being deemed unsafe as in *R v Taylor and Taylor* (1994) 98 Cr App R 361
Panel of 12 • Seen to be fairer • A wider set of experiences represented • Prevents bias • Can establish, for example, dishonesty and reasonableness on the standards of ordinary people	**Perverse verdicts** • At times the jury can refuse to follow the law and convict a defendant e.g. in *R v Kronlid and others* (1996) *The Times* 10th September
	Fraud trials • These can be extremely long and complex however, under s 43 Criminal Justice Act 2003 (not yet in force), the prosecution can apply for trial by a sole judge in complex cases • Robert Julian (2007) found judges were more likely to agree with a jury verdict in serious fraud cases than in others
	High acquittal rates • It is assumed that juries are more likely to acquit • However, research in 2008 found that of the cases in which juries are required to decide the verdict, they acquitted only in 30% of cases
	Other disadvantages • Compulsory service • Potential for jury tampering • Slow and expensive procedure

8.8.3 Alternatives to jury trials

Trial by a single judge	A panel of judges
Regarded as fairer, used in criminal cases in N. Ireland. Less potential for tampering. Less public confidence, elitist. Individual prejudices have more impact	Occurs in some European countries. Could be seen to be too removed from the people, requires more judges, therefore could be expensive

Judge plus lay assessors	A mini-jury of 6
Used in Scandinavian countries. Combines legal expertise with public input. Could include special assessors in fraud cases	Juries of 9 used in some European countries. Could be used for less serious cases. Cheaper

Workpoint

Put yourself in the shoes of a defendant in a case triable either way. Would you want to be tried by judge and jury or by magistrates? Give reasons for your answer.

Checkpoint

Task	Done
I know the history behind the development of the jury system	
I understand who can act as a juror	
I understand the reasons why a juror may be disqualified	
I know how an individual can be excused from jury service	
I know the procedure for selecting jurors in court and the vetting system	
I know how juries are used in civil cases	
I know how juries are used in Coroners' Courts	
I know how juries are used in criminal cases and the rules relating to secrecy in the jury room	
I know key research findings into the use of juries	
I can analyse the advantages and disadvantages of jury trials	

Potential exam questions

1) Describe how the system of jury trials developed and how they are used in the modern court system.
2) Who can become a juror and how are they selected?
3) What are the advantages and disadvantages of jury trials?

Chapter 9
Lay Magistrates

9.1 Introduction

> **Definition**
>
> *Lay people*: People who are not legally qualified.

Lay people are used in the legal system as:

• Juries

• Panels in the Patent Court and the Admiralty Court

• However, they are most prominent in the Magistrates' Court as lay magistrates.

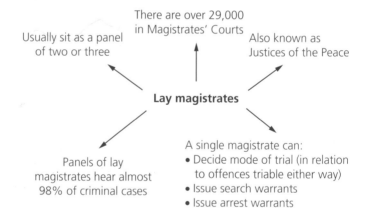

Lay magistrates are not district judges. District judges are **qualified** judges who work in Magistrates' Courts. They used to be called stipendiary magistrates.

Section 16(3) of the Justices of the Peace Act 1979:

Has the same powers as…

District judge = **Panel of magistrates**

Workpoint

Do you think that it is acceptable that people without legal training should have such a large role in the English legal system, particularly in relation to criminal cases?

9.2 History of the Magistracy: Timeline

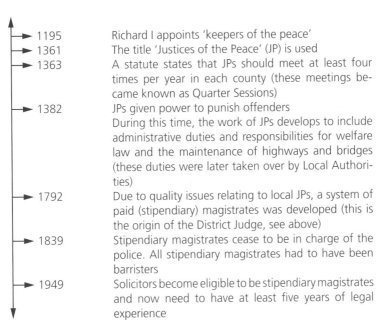

1195	Richard I appoints 'keepers of the peace'
1361	The title 'Justices of the Peace' (JP) is used
1363	A statute states that JPs should meet at least four times per year in each county (these meetings became known as Quarter Sessions)
1382	JPs given power to punish offenders
	During this time, the work of JPs develops to include administrative duties and responsibilities for welfare law and the maintenance of highways and bridges (these duties were later taken over by Local Authorities)
1792	Due to quality issues relating to local JPs, a system of paid (stipendiary) magistrates was developed (this is the origin of the District Judge, see above)
1839	Stipendiary magistrates cease to be in charge of the police. All stipendiary magistrates had to have been barristers
1949	Solicitors become eligible to be stipendiary magistrates and now need to have at least five years of legal experience

9.3 Qualifications for Lay Magistrates

There are **no** formal qualifications required **but** the following rules apply to **serving as a magistrate** and therefore becoming a member of the Bench:

Age:

From 18–65 (increased from 60 in 2000).

Limitations:

• Should be 'of good standing'.

• No **serious** criminal convictions.

• Undischarged bankrupts are disqualified.

They need to commit to at least 26 half-days a year.

They are expected to live or work within the relevant local justice area.

Ineligible:

- Those involved in law enforcement.
- Members of the armed forces.
- Close relatives of those employed in the criminal justice system in the local area.
- Two close relatives will not be employed on the same bench.

Allowed to claim the following **actual** allowances:

- Travel.
- Subsistence.
- Financial loss.

Social awareness Good character Understanding and communication

Personal qualities of a magistrate

Sound judgement Commitment and reliability Maturity and sound temperament

---

Workpoint

Think of yourself and those you know. Who do you think would make a good magistrate and why? Would the people who you believe could make a good magistrate have the time and resources to commit to the role?

9.4 Selection and Appointment of Lay Magistrates

- From **1,700–2,200** appointed each year.
- Appointments are made by the Lord Chancellor '*on behalf of and in the name of Her Majesty*'.
- Advisory Committees recommend candidates for appointment.

- The National Strategy for Recruitment of Lay Magistrates (2003) aims to achieve:

  - Better representation

  - A socially diverse Bench

  - Flexibility to encourage those with other responsibilities to sit

  - Co-operation with employers

  - Revision of recruitment methods.

There were only **two high priority** actions:

1. Campaigns aimed at employers to reduce the employment impact on magistrates.

2. Recruitment campaigns using a variety of media.

9.4.1 The procedure of Advisory Panels

- Encouragement of applications – nomination or direct applications

- First interview: Based on the six personal qualities above

- Second interview: Examines candidates' potential judicial aptitude

- Assessment of whether the Bench reflects the community, taking into account:

  - Gender

  - Ethnic origin

  - Geographical spread

  - Occupation

  - But *not* political affiliation.

Key aim:

The Bench represents all aspects of society.

> **Workpoint**
>
> In order to achieve justice, to what extent do you believe that magistrates should be representative of the country as a whole? Think about the system of appointing magistrates and their role. What barriers do you think could exist to achieving full representation?

9.5 Training of Lay Magistrates

Training is carried out by the Magistrates' Committee of the Judicial Studies Board. Forty-two unified areas are overseen by the Ministry of Justice.

Training takes place under four areas of competence under the Magistrates' National Training Initiative 2004 (MNTI2):

1. Managing yourself

2. Working as a team

3. Making judicial decisions

4. Managing judicial decision-making (only applies to the chairperson of the Bench).

New magistrates undertake:

1. Initial training

2. Core training which develops key skills

3. Activities such as observations.

This training process is aided by:

• The appointment of mentors

• Attendance at training sessions

• Appraisals – after two years then at least once every three years

• Post-sitting reviews

• The creation of a focus on **equality** of treatment.

9.6 Resignation and Removal of Lay Justices

9.6.1 Courts Act 2003 s 11

9.6.1.1 Resignation

Magistrates must retire at age **70**.

9.6.1.2 Removal

The Lord Chancellor can remove a magistrate due to:

- Incapacity (including illness) or misbehaviour (e.g. conviction for an offence).

- Persistent failure to meet standards of competence (as reinforced by MNTI2 – see above).

- Failure to take proper part in the exercise of the role's functions (e.g. not attending the required number of sittings).

9.7 Magistrates' Duties

Criminal cases
Magistrates:
<ul><li>Try 98% of cases</li><li>Decide guilt</li><li>Pass sentence:<ul><li>6 months' imprisonment for a single offence (Criminal Justice Act 2003 will allow for 12 months if it comes into force)</li><li>12 months' imprisonment for two or more offences (Criminal Justice Act 2003 will allow for 15 months if it comes into force)</li></ul></li><li>Deal with preliminary matters such as early administrative hearings and bail applications</li><li>Deal with young (between 10 and 17 years old) offenders in the Youth Court</li></ul>
Civil cases
Magistrates deal with matters such as:
<ul><li>Enforcement of debts in relation to utilities (e.g. gas, electricity, water)</li><li>Non-payment of council tax and television licences</li><li>Appeals from the refusal of a licence to sell alcohol</li></ul>
Family cases
Magistrates with special training deal with matters such as:
<ul><li>Domestic violence orders</li><li>Adoption orders</li><li>Proceedings under the Children Act 1989 relating to, for example, residence and contact in relation to children</li></ul>

9.8 The Magistrates' Clerk

Each Bench has a clerk (legal adviser) and the senior clerk has to be qualified as a barrister or solicitor for at least five years.

The magistrates' clerk (or legal adviser):

- Has a duty to guide the magistrates on questions of law, practice and procedure.

- Has to be legally qualified (since 2010).

- Since a Practice Direction of 2000 has to give legal advice in open court.

- Has a role defined by the Justices' Clerks Rules 1999 (SI No 2784).

- Has powers to issue warrants for arrest, extend bail and adjourn criminal proceedings in certain circumstances.

9.9 Advantages and Disadvantages of using Lay Magistrates

Advantages	Disadvantages
Representation • Good gender/ethnic split (perhaps due to advertising campaigns) • Better representation than District Judges	**Representation** • Professional and managerial classes, and the retired are over-represented, they are seen to be middle-aged and middle-class • Very few under the age of 40 • However, the representation is better than District Judges
Local knowledge • It is envisaged magistrates continue to have a link to the area within 15 miles of where they sit. • They should have a good understanding of local issues and attitudes. However, given the representation of professional classes there may be less knowledge of poorer areas. • Increased centralisation of magistrates' courts means that the impact of local knowledge is diminished.	**Prosecution bias** • It is suspected that magistrates are too ready to believe the police or the CPS representative with whom they build up a relationship. This is being addressed in training. • There is a lower acquittal rate which may be due to a prosecution bias.

Advantages	Disadvantages
Cost • Much cheaper than District Judges (approx. several millions of pounds per year). • Cost of magistrates' trials is much cheaper than the Crown Court.	Inconsistency in sentencing • Geographical disparities in sentencing and in charging.
Legal expertise: • Since 2010, legal advisers have to be legally qualified which increases legal expertise in the court. • MNTI2 improves the training of magistrates, as does the role of the Judicial Studies Board.	Reliance on the clerk • The clerk can give legal advice but not aid in sentencing, too much reliance on a clerk may lead to inconsistencies.
Fewer appeals • Approx. 5,000 appeals against conviction a year, with around 2,000 allowed. • Approx. 6,000–7,000 appeals against sentence a year with 3,000–3,500 allowed. • Approx. 100 appeals on a point of law to the Queen's Bench Divisional Court a year with 50 allowed. • Given the amount of cases these courts hear (approx. two million a year), these are very small numbers.	

Workpoint

If you were developing a country's legal system from scratch, would you include a role for lay magistrates? If so, what would their role entail and how would they be trained?

Research Point

Take a look at the DirectGov website www.direct.gov.uk and search for 'volunteer as a magistrate'. Do you think that this information encourages people to apply to be a magistrate? Does it give an effective overview of the role of a magistrate?

Checkpoint

Task	Done
I can explain what a magistrate is	
I understand the role of magistrates in the English legal system	
I can outline the history of the magistracy	
I can explain what qualifications are needed to be a magistrate	
I know how magistrates are selected and appointed	
I understand the nature of the training required to be a magistrate	
I know the reasons why magistrates can be removed from post	
I understand the role of the magistrates' clerk	
I can evaluate the advantages and disadvantages of the use of lay magistrates	

Potential exam questions

1) Describe how the system of lay magistrates developed and how they are used in the modern court system.
2) How are lay magistrates selected and trained?
3) What are the advantages and disadvantages of jury trials?

Chapter 10
The Legal Profession

10.1 Introduction

The word **lawyer** usually refers to solicitors and barristers. The distinction, however, between these two roles is now blurred. See 10.2, below, on rights of audience.

Other legal roles include:

• Qualified legal executives

• Licensed conveyancers

• Notaries

• Legal clerks

• Paralegals.

Definitions

ILEX: The Institute of Legal Executives, the awarding body for fully qualified legal executives. Fellowship of the Institute is a free-standing legal qualification. It has 22,000 members.

Paralegal: A general term to describe personnel who work in the legal field. They may or may not have formal legal qualifications. ILEX offers a recognised paralegal qualification. Paralegals may or may not attend court and may or may not be fee earners.

10.1.1 How to become a solicitor

Law degree route (55% of solicitors)	Non-law degree route	Fellow of ILEX route
Law degree	Degree in any subject	ILEX Professional Diploma and employment in a firm
	Graduate Diploma in Law	ILEX Higher Professional Diploma and employment in a firm
Student membership of the Law Society	Student membership of the Law Society	Fellowship of ILEX
Legal Practice Course: This focuses on practical aspects of the work	Legal Practice Course: This focuses on practical aspects of the work	Legal Practice Course: This focuses on practical aspects of the work
Training Contract: Salaried training attached to a practising solicitor	Training Contract:Salaried training attached to a practising solicitor	ILEX Fellows are exempt from the Training Contract due to employment experience
Professional Skills Course	Professional Skills Course	Professional Skills Course
Admission to the profession of solicitor through entrance on the Roll of Officers of the Supreme Court	Admission to the profession of solicitor through entrance on the Roll of Officers of the Supreme Court	Admission to the profession of solicitor through entrance on the Roll of Officers of the Supreme Court

10.1.1.1 Other methods

Transfer

- Overseas lawyers

- Barrister

- Scottish/Northern Ireland lawyers

Other

- Justices' clerk (a magistrates' court clerk of at least five years' standing who passes the LPC)

10.2 Solicitors

- Governing body is The Law Society of England and Wales under the amended Solicitors Act 1974.

- Many solicitors form **partnerships** as firms.

10.2.1 Who are solicitors?

Some statistics from the Law Society's most recent Annual Statistical Report found at www.lawsociety.org.uk/aboutlawsociety/whatwedo/researchandtrends/statisticalreport.law are shown below.

In 2009–10:

45.8% of solicitors with practising certificates were women.
11.9% of all solicitors on the Roll, **11.1%** of all solicitors with practising certificates, and **10.3%** of all solicitors in private practice were from Black Minority and Ethnic groups.
76.3% of men holding practising certificates work within private practice, compared to **70.4%** of women.
The average age of a male practising certificate holder was **44.4** years compared to **38.1** years for female practising certificate holders.
The average age of a female solicitor in private practice was **37.5** years compared with **44.7** years for men.
The average age of a sole practitioner was **50.0** years compared with **47.5** years for partners and **41.5** years for all solicitors in private practice.
Over one-third of practising certificate holders **(37.2%)** were employed by organisations based in London.

Research Point

Access the Executive Summaries of the Law Society's Annual Statistical Report on the link given above. What sort of trends can you see arising in the profession?

10.2.2 What do solicitors do?

- Provide legal services on a face-to-face basis, by letter or by telephone.

- Many specialise in legal areas with popular ones being:

  - Business affairs

  - Litigation – commercial and general

  - Residential conveyancing

  - Wills and probate

  - Employment

  - Family

The Courts and Legal Services Act (CLSA) 1990

- Aimed to improve the delivery of legal services to the public.
- Opened up the sphere to those other than solicitors and barristers.
- Increased competition.
- Provided that non-solicitors involved in conveyancing work (as established under Part II of the Administration of Justice Act 1985) are suitably qualified, accountable and insured.

Rights of Audience

- Before 1993, only barristers were allowed to appear and conduct proceedings in the High Court, Court of Appeal and House of Lords (and they had nearly all of the rights of audience in the Crown Court).
- The CLSA 1990 created a system to grant rights of audience through a Certificate of Advocacy. The holders of these Higher Rights Certificates are known as solicitor-advocates. There are three types of certificate:

Higher Courts	Higher Courts	Higher Courts
(All proceedings)	(Civil proceedings)	(Criminal proceedings)
(Civil and criminal advocacy)	(Civil advocacy)	(Criminal advocacy)

Since 2007 the following routes to becoming a solicitor-advocate exist:

1. Development route
2. Accreditation route
3. Exemption route
4. Former barrister route

Initially only independent solicitors could apply for the Certificates but since 1997 employed solicitors can now do so. Solicitor-advocates (alongside barristers) can be appointed as Queen's Counsel (QC) – see 10.3.2 below.

10.2.3 Who regulates complaints about the legal profession?

The profession is self-regulatory. Since the Legal Services Act 2007, the functions of governing bodies have been split as follows:

	Solicitors	Barristers
Representative body	The Law Society	The Bar Council
Regulatory body	The Solicitors Regulation Authority	The Bar Standards Board
Complaints handling body	Legal Complaints Service	The Bar Standards Board

Making a complaint against a solicitor

First: Use the firm's in-house complaints procedure:

↓

Under the Solicitors' Code of Conduct, each firm needs to have an in-house procedure for dealing with complaints. This must include a written complaints procedure and strategies to keep the client informed of both the procedures and the development of the complaint.

↓

If this does not produce a satisfactory result, approach **The Law Society**:

Poor service or billing issues	are dealt with by	The Office for Legal Complaints
Issues of standards	are dealt with by	The Solicitors Regulation Authority

↓

The SRA can close down a firm or refer the matter to **The Solicitors Disciplinary Tribunal**:

This operates under the amended Solicitors Act 1974 and adjudicates on matters of misconduct or breach of professional rules. Its powers include:

Striking off   Suspension   Reprimanding   Fining   Banning

↓

The final port of call is **The Office of the Legal Services Ombudsman**.

This office:
- Ensures that the professional bodies deal with complaints effectively.
- Ensures that standards are upheld.
- Seeks to raise standards in the complaints system.
- Can recommend that a professional body reconsiders a complaint.
- Recommends the payment of damages based on distress or inconvenience.

Definition

> Professional indemnity insurance: The insurance that all solicitors in private practice need to hold in case of a finding of negligent loss to a client.

10.3 Barristers

A practising barrister must belong to one of the four Inns of Court (and eat a number of dinners there):

- Inner Temple
- Middle Temple
- Lincoln's Inn
- Gray's Inn.

Definition

> 'Call to the Bar': The procedure (managed by the four Inns of Court above) by which students become barristers.

Workpoint

Look earlier in this chapter and find the name of barristers':

1. Regulatory body

2. Representative body

In 2010:

- 80% of barristers are self-employed. Those not self-employed can work in, for example, commerce, industry, government or solicitors' firms.
- 31.5% of self-employed barristers were female.
- 9.6% self-employed barristers stated that they were a member of an ethnic minority.

Workpoint

Access the website of the Bar Council at www.barcouncil.org.uk. Look at the section 'About barristers' and then 'statistics' and access the report 'The Bar Barometer'. Compare these figures to the research above in relation to solicitors. Are there any significant differences between the composition of barristers and solicitors?

Barristers **do not** form partnerships but the majority join **chambers**.

> **Chambers**
> - 60% are in London.
> - Act as a way of allowing barristers to share resources e.g. a clerk.
> - Employ one or more clerks who allocate work and arrange fees.

10.3.1 Becoming a barrister

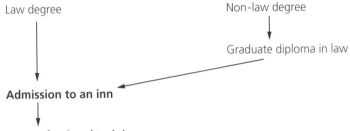

Law degree

Non-law degree

Graduate diploma in law

Admission to an inn

Bar professional training course
Skills-based course with modules on case preparation, research, written skills, opinion-writing, drafting, conference skills, negotiation, advocacy and subject-specific modules.

Pupillage
One year practical, salaried training alongside a practising barrister. It includes:

- six months of 'non-practising' work through shadowing
- six months of practising work such as giving legal advice and exercising rights of audience.

Tenancy
A place in chambers to work as a fully qualified barrister.

> **How are barristers accessed?**
> - In the past they always received instructions from a solicitor.
> - Currently through 'Licensed Access', organisations such as the police and trade unions can have direct access.
> - Since 2002, 'Public Access' allows a member of the public to directly instruct a barrister (but not in the case of most criminal, family, immigration and asylum work).
>   - Advantage: The process becomes much cheaper.
>   - Disadvantage: The public may not approach the most appropriate chambers.

Definition

> The cab-rank rule: Under paragraph 2 of the Code of Conduct of the Bar of England and Wales, a barrister must accept the brief which they are assigned and cannot refuse to provide services (this does not apply to the Public Access scheme)

Workpoint

Think about how a citizen's right to access justice could be affected if the cab-rank rule did not exist. To what extent do you believe that the rule is necessary?

10.3.2 Queen's Counsel (QC)

- Becoming a QC is known as 'taking silk'.
- QCs wear a silk gown, sit in the court's front row, are invited to speak first and tend to specialise in a particular area.
- Most High Court judges are appointed from QCs.
- The selection process has been reformed (and may be again) due to a lack of transparency.

10.3.3 Making a complaint against a barrister

The process is regulated by the Code of Conduct of the Bar of England and Wales.

First: Approach the solicitor who directed the barrister (if the barrister was not accessed directly)

↓

Next: Approach the barrister to try to resolve the issue

↓

If there is no resolution: Approach the Bar Standards Board (BSB). The BSB's complaints procedure is overseen by the Complaints Commissioner. The Board has the power to:

- Request that the barrister apologise to the client
- Disbar the barrister
- Suspend the barrister
- Fine the barrister
- Order that fees be repaid

↓

Finally: If the matter is not resolved then the Office for Legal Complaints can be approached. The Legal Ombudsman tries to informally resolve the case and can issue orders for compensation.

Case:	
Arthur J S Hall v Simons (2000)	Removed an historic immunity from actions for negligence enjoyed by barristers (and solicitor-advocates). The immunity was no longer in the public interest and was not reflected in other professions.

Research Point

Access the website of the Office for Legal Complaints' Legal Ombudsman: www.legalombudsman.org.uk. Take a look at the work carried out and the outlines of the decisions. To what extent do you think that the Office provides an effective and necessary service?

10.4 The Future for the Legal Profession: Where Next?

10.4.1 Fusion

Why is there a need for a division between solicitors and barristers? Why can't there just be one role of 'lawyer'?

Advantages of fusion:

- Removes the need to employ a solicitor and a barrister.
- Would be cheaper, more efficient and would remove communications delays.

Disadvantages of fusion:

- A split profession increases free market competition and consumer choice.
- The competition provided by a split profession keeps costs down.
- The cab-rank rule in relation to barristers ensures that all who need representation can have access to it without the need for fusion.

The professional bodies have been consistently **opposed** to fusion.

Workpoint

Do you believe that, given the blurring between the roles of solicitors and barristers, the two roles should be fused? Give reasons for your answer.

10.4.2 The Legal Services Act 2007 and Alternative Business Structures (ABSs)

Definition

> Alternative Business Structures: A business structure, provision for which is contained in the Legal Services Act 2007, in which legal professionals form partnerships with non-lawyers such as accountants, tax consultants and estate agents.

ABSs would allow for more than 25% of the organisation to comprise non-legal personnel and may permit sole external ownership. This significantly transforms the traditional restrictions on the business structures available to solicitors and barristers.

Aim of ABSs

To provide a consolidated 'one-stop shop' providing professional services.

Advantages	Disadvantages
Direct access, convenience, consumer choice, professional choice	Loss of the legal profession's independence, concentration of high-quality professionals thereby reducing choice, potential for conflicts of interest, issues of confidentiality and professional privilege, difficulty regulating professional conduct

Workpoint

If you were to buy a house, would you prefer that your estate agent, surveyor and conveyancer were all part of the same organisation with one main contact point? Give reasons for your answer.

Checkpoint

Task	Done
I can outline the different roles undertaken in the legal profession	
I understand the ways in which an individual can qualify to be a solicitor	

Checkpoint (continued)

Task	Done
I can describe the composition of the occupation of solicitor	
I can outline the work of solicitors	
I know how solicitors can now be granted rights of audience	
I can outline the procedure for making a complaint against a solicitor	
I know the names of the different bodies which regulate and represent both barristers and solicitors	
I understand the ways in which an individual can become a barrister	
I can describe the composition of the occupation of barrister	
I can outline how barristers work and understand the cab-rank rule	
I know what a QC is and can outline who can become a QC	
I can outline the procedure for making a complaint against a barrister and whether they can be found liable for professional negligence	
I can analyse the advantages and disadvantages of fusion in the legal profession	
I can analyse the impact of Alternative Business Structures on the legal profession	

Potential exam questions

1) What are the routes to becoming a solicitor and what sort of work do they undertake?
2) What are the routes to becoming a barrister and what sort of work do they undertake?
3) What is fusion? What are the advantages and disadvantages of fusion?
4) In relation to the legal profession, what are Alternative Business Structures and do you think that they are a good idea?

Chapter 11
The Judiciary

11.1 Introduction

Judges:

- Arbitrate disputes

- Make decisions on the law

- Make decisions on fact (the majority of cases do not use juries)

- Are appointed by the Queen

- Used to be appointed on advice from the Lord Chancellor.

However, changes to the role of the Lord Chancellor were enacted by the Constitutional Reform Act 2005.

Before the Constitutional Reform Act 2005, the Lord Chancellor was:

- Head of the Judiciary (this is now the Lord Chief Justice, judicial appointments are now dealt with by the Judicial Appointments Commission)

- A judge in the House of Lords and the High Court (Chancery Division).

The Lord Chancellor continues to:

- Hold responsibility (alongside the Ministry of Justice) for how the court system operates)

- Sit as a member of the Cabinet (Executive) appointed by the Prime Minister.

Since the Constitutional Reform Act 2005, the Lord Chancellor can be appointed from the House of Lords or the House of Commons.

Workpoint

Consider how the role of the Lord Chancellor before the Constitutional Reform Act 2005 conflicted with the concept of the separation of powers.

The Constitutional Reform Act 2005 also established the Supreme Court. This:

- Replaced the Appellate Committee of the House of Lords but sits with the same judges.

- Has the same jurisdiction as the Appellate Committee of the House of Lords but now covers the devolution issues previously addressed by the Privy Council.

- Opened in October 2009.

- Increases the separation of powers as it removes the judiciary's proximity to the House of Lords (the chamber of Parliament).

- Does not have the power to strike down legislation.

11.2 The Judicial Hierarchy

11.2.1 Senior judges

Court	Judge	Judges' qualifications
The Supreme Court (and Privy Council)	Justice of the Supreme Court	Two years in a high judicial office (superior court)
The Court of Appeal	Lord or Lady Justice of Appeal	Appointed from High Court judges
	Head of Division	Appointed from Lords Justices of Appeal
The High Court	High Court Judge (can also sit in the Crown Court)	Seven-year High Court qualification

11.2.2 Inferior judges

Court	Judge	Judges' qualifications
The Crown Court	Circuit Judge	Seven-year general qualification or three years as a district judge
	Recorder	Seven-year general qualification

Court	Judge	Judges' qualifications
County Court	Circuit Judge	Seven-year general qualification or three years as a district judge
	Recorder	Seven-year general qualification
	District Judge	Five-year general qualification
Magistrates' Court	District Judge	Five-year general qualification or ILEX Fellowship (under Tribunals, Courts and Enforcement Act 2007)

11.3 Training

Definition

Judicial Studies Board (JSB): The organisation, established in 1978, which provides judicial training and advises on the training of lay magistrates and tribunal personnel. It:

- Organises refresher sessions

- Highlights areas of change or current interest

- Publishes books and guidance.

11.4 Appointments of Inferior Judges

Appointments are governed by the Courts and Legal Services Act 1990.

The Judicial Appointments Commission (JAC) makes recommendations on merit looking at:

*Intellectual capacity   *Personal qualities   *Equality of approach

*Authority and communication   *Efficiency
 skills

↓

The selections made by the JAC are
given to the Lord Chancellor
who can accept or reject them

↓

The Queen appoints judges

11.4.1 Different types of inferior judges

Circuit judges

- Need to be qualified barristers or solicitors with seven years of legal experience or be a Recorder or be holder of a full-time judicial office for at least three years.

- They are permanently assigned to one of the six circuits.

Recorders

- Need to be qualified barristers or solicitors with seven years of legal experience.

- They are part-time judges, appointed for five years which is usually extended in further five-year terms.

- They retire at 65.

District judges (Civil Court)

- These comprise the majority of District Judges known as Registrars.

- They need to be qualified barristers or solicitors with five years of legal experience.

- They usually will have sat as a part-time Deputy District Judge for at least two years.

District judges (Magistrates' Court)

- Must have been qualified for five years.

- They usually have been a part-time Deputy District Judge previously.

- ILEX Fellows can now be appointed to this post.

11.4.2 Different types of superior judges

Justices of the Supreme Court

- Need to have held one or more of the judicial offices outlined in the Appellate Jurisdiction Act 1876.

- They are usually the most experienced judges from the Court of Appeal, the Court of Session in Scotland and the Court of Appeal in Northern Ireland.

- Appointments are made by the Queen on the advice of the Prime Minister and Lord Chancellor.

Figure continued overleaf

The Five Heads of Division

- Appointed under ss 65–75 of the Constitutional Reform Act 2005 (CRA).

- Chosen from the Justices of the Supreme Court or Lord Justices of Appeal.

Lord Justice of Appeal

- There are 37, appointed by the Queen following ss 76–85 of the CRA 2005 on the advice of the Lord Chancellor, under advice from a selection panel.

- Need to be qualified as a barrister or solicitor for at least seven years or be a High Court judge.

High Court judges

- Appointed by the Queen under Advice from the Lord Chancellor following a recommendation from Judicial Appointments Commission under ss 76–84 of the CRA 2005.

- They can also work in the Crown Court and the Court of Appeal.

- They need to be qualified as a barrister or solicitor for at least seven years or have been a Circuit Judge for at least two years.

- QCs are often appointed.

11.5 Judicial Appointments

Some have commentated that has been a lack of transparency and a perceived nepotism in judicial appointments.

This has been addressed by the creation and role of the Judicial Appointments Commission. However, judges in the Court of Appeal and Supreme Court are appointed by invitation only and vacancies do not have to be advertised.

Research Point

Imagine that you have a friend who works as a lawyer in a foreign country who asks you how you become one of the highest judges in England and Wales. Using the material here and your own further research, explain to your friend the process by which this could be achieved.

11.6 The Composition of the Judiciary

Commentators have noted that judges may not be representative of society as they are mostly elderly, Oxbridge-educated males.

Some statistics from 2011

- 5.1% of all judges are from a black and ethnic minority background. None of these sits in the Supreme Court, Court of Appeal or are Heads of Division.

- 22.3% of all judges are female, this includes one of the twelve Justices of the Supreme Court and four of the 37 Lord Justices of Appeal.

Workpoint

To what extent do you believe that having a representative judiciary is essential to an effective and fair judicial system?

11.7 Dismissal and Judicial Independence

Judges can leave post due to:

Retirement

- This must be before a judge reaches his or her seventieth birthday (under the Judicial Pensions and Retirement Act 1993).

- Judges need to serve for twenty years to receive a full pension.

Dismissal

See table below for a summary of the conditions for dismissal.

Justices of the Supreme Court, Heads of Division, Lords Justices of Appeal, High Court Judges	Inferior Judges
• Can only be removed by the Queen after a vote of both chambers of Parliament. To date, this has never happened.	• Can be dismissed on grounds of incapacity or misbehaviour by the Lord Chief Justice without the need for Parliament's authority.

Justices of the Supreme Court, Heads of Division, Lords Justices of Appeal, High Court Judges	Inferior Judges
• Governed by the Senior Courts Act 1981.	• The terms of service for those on fixed-term contracts include provisions not to renew on grounds of, for example, misbehaviour or incapacity.

Definition

The Office for Judicial Complaints: An organisation established under the CRA 2005 with the power to investigate complaints about judges. These complaints, however, need to be upheld by the Lord Chancellor and Lord Chief Justice.

11.7.1 Judicial impartiality

Judges must be seen to be **independent** from the other arms of State and the parties in the cases he or she is hearing.

Cases in which potential judicial bias was found:

Case:	
R v Bow Street Metropolitan Stipendiary Magistrate and Others ex parte Pinochet Ugarte (No 2) (1999)	The decision taken not to quash General Pinochet's extradition warrants was itself quashed as Lord Hoffman (a judge in the House of Lords case) did not withdraw or declare an affiliation with Amnesty International (a party represented in the case).
Timmins v Gormley (2000)	The judge had written a number of articles in which he criticised a firm of insurers who were then defendants in a case he heard.

General issues

- Judges should treat **all** equally.

- Judges should disclose **any** interest in the outcome of the case as soon as possible.

Workpoint

Remember that the qualities the Judicial Appointments Commission apply in the recommendation of an individual for a judicial post:

- Intellectual capacity

- Personal qualities (integrity, sound judgement, decisiveness, objectivity, willingness to learn)

- Equality of approach

- Authority and communication skills

- Efficiency.

Do you believe that any of these qualities are more important than others? Do you believe that any arbitrator can take a truly equal approach in all cases?

Checkpoint

Task	Done
I can explain how the role of the Lord Chancellor in relation to the judiciary has been reformed	
I can describe the judicial hierarchy and which judges sit in which courts	
I can outline the role of the Judicial Studies Board	
I know how inferior judges are appointed	
I know how superior judges are appointed	
I can outline why there were changes to the system of judicial appointments	
I can describe key issues in relation to the representativeness of the judiciary	
I know how judges can leave a post	
I understand the rules on judicial impartiality	

Potential exam questions

1) What impact did the Constitutional Reform Act of 2005 have on the judiciary?
2) How are judges appointed and trained?
3) What criticisms can be made of the composition of the judiciary and to what extent are they being addressed?

Chapter 12
Sentencing

12.1 Introduction

- On a plea or finding of guilt, a court will impose a sentence or give an absolute or conditional discharge.

- Sentences include:

  - Imprisonment

  - Fines

  - Community orders.

- Magistrates operate under some sentencing restrictions:

  - usually up to six months' imprisonment or a £5,000 fine.

- The Crown Court has no limits:

  - they can impose life imprisonment and there is no maximum fine.

12.1.1 Key sentencing issues

- Some crimes have fixed maximum sentences (e.g. theft = seven years).

- Some such as rape and manslaughter have a maximum sentence of life, giving judges full sentencing discretion.

- Murder has a **mandatory** life sentence, judges have no choice but to impose life imprisonment.

- Minimum sentences apply for three offences:

  - Burglary (three years if it is a third or further offence)

  - Class A Drug Trafficking (seven years if it is a third or further offence)

  - Possession of Prohibited Firearms (five years, even if it is a first offence).

- The Criminal Justice Act 2003 allows the Crown Court to impose an indeterminate sentence on a dangerous offender for public protection. It also allows for an extension period to be imposed on top of a maximum sentence which can **only** be used where the court finds the defendant to pose a significant risk of serious harm to the public.

- Specific rules govern the sentences available to be imposed on young offenders.

12.2 Purposes of Sentencing

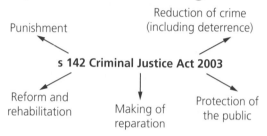

Punishment

Reduction of crime (including deterrence)

s 142 Criminal Justice Act 2003

Reform and rehabilitation

Making of reparation

Protection of the public

> **Criminal Justice Act 2003**
> *Section 142*
>
> *(1) Any court dealing with an offender in respect of his offence must have regard to the following purposes of sentencing—*
>
> *(a) the punishment of offenders,*
>
> *(b) the reduction of crime (including its reduction by deterrence),*
>
> *(c) the reform and rehabilitation of offenders,*
>
> *(d) the protection of the public, and*
>
> *(e) the making of reparation by offenders to persons affected by their offences.*

Workpoint

Take a look at the figure illustrating the purposes of sentencing above. In the statute they have no hierarchy of importance but can you place them in the order of how important you believe them to be. You may have to look at the table below for further explanation. Give reasons for the approach you take.

Principal aim: Prevention of offending
by those under 18

s 142 A Criminal Justice Act 2003: Purposes of sentencing:

Punishment   Reform and   Protection of   Reparation
                    Rehabilitation   the public

**The approach taken with young
offenders (under 18)**

s 44 Children and Young Persons Act 1933:

The court should also have regard to the welfare of the young person.

12.2.1 Punishment

- Also known as retribution.

- Based on the offender deserving punishment.

- Does not look to reduce future offending.

- Imposes a sentence in proportion to the offender's act.

- Under the Coroners and Justice Act 2009, the Sentencing Council of England and Wales produces general principles for sentencing.

- The guidelines can focus on certain aspects of a crime, e.g. use or threat of force, or use of a weapon.

- Courts will have to impose sentences within the offence range unless the case is exceptional.

- The impact of the guidelines on resources has to be assessed.

12.2.1.1 Advantages of this system

- Achieves retribution.

- Achieves consistency.

12.2.1.2 Disadvantages of this system

- Removes judicial discretion.

- Is too rigid and overlooks mitigation.

- Ignores the needs of the offender.

12.2.2 Deterrence

Individual

- Aims to ensure that the actual defender does not re-offend.

- Prison does not appear to deter, particularly in relation to young people.

- The approach overlooks the opportunistic nature of criminal activity.

- Fear of being caught could be more of a deterrent.

General

- Aims to ensure that **other** offenders do not commit crime.

- Used to warn others of the sentence they could face.

- Often used when a particular crime has become more prevalent.

- Conflicts with the principle of proportionate retribution.

12.2.3 Reform and rehabilitation

- Looks forward to alter the behaviour of the offender and reduce future crime.

- Community sentences focus on this aim.

- Issues such as job prospects and medical reports can be taken into account.

- Sentences can be more individualised: this could be inconsistent and tends to discriminate against poorer offenders.

12.2.4 Protection of the public

- Through incapacitation, the offender is prevented from reoffending.

- Long prison sentences achieve this aim particularly in the case of dangerous offenders.

- Driving bans, curfews and exclusion orders can achieve this aim.

12.2.5 Reparation

- Aims to help the offender repair links with society and/or the victim.

- Found in the court's powers to order compensation.

- Includes community sentences with work on community projects.

- Restorative justice aims to give the offender an understanding of the impact of the crime by, for example, bringing the offender face-to-face with the victim.

12.2.6 Denunciation

This is not specifically mentioned in the Criminal Justice Act 2003.

- Through punishment, society expresses its disapproval with criminal behaviour.
- This highlights society's moral boundaries and the nature of acceptable conduct.

Workpoint

Imagine that you are a judge and, after a period of nationwide violent unrest, a defendant is brought before you on charges relating to criminal damage and looting. Take each of the aims of punishment in turn and outline the sentence you would impose, justifying it on the basis of the aim. Look back at your list, which sentence do you think you would actually impose?

Research Point

Take a look at the website of the Sentencing Council of England and Wales: http://sentencingcouncil.judiciary.gov.uk. To what extent do you believe that it will be effective in achieving consistency of sentencing?

12.3 Custodial Sentences

These are the most serious punishment a court can impose.

12.3.1 Life sentences

Mandatory life sentence

- Has to be imposed where a person over 21 has pleaded or is found guilty on a charge of murder.
- This is not incompatible with Articles 3 (torture) and 5 (liberty) of the ECHR.
- The judge, following s 269 of the Criminal Justice Act 2003, sets a minimum period to be served within the boundaries of full life down to 12 years.
- Whole life should be set if:
  - Two or more people have been murdered with premeditation or sadistic conduct.
  - A child has been murdered following abduction or with sadistic motivation.
  - The murder advances a political, religious or ideological cause.
  - The offender had been previously convicted of murder.

Aggravating and mitigating factors

Aggravating factors include:

- Vulnerability of the victim and any physical or mental suffering inflicted.

Mitigating factors include:

- The offender's intention to cause GBH rather than death, lack of pre-meditation, some evidence of acting in self-defence.

Indeterminate sentence for public protection

- Under s 225 CJA 2003 this sentence can be imposed on those convicted of a serious offence where there is deemed a significant risk to the public of serious harm.

- A minimum period after which a parole hearing can take place will be set.

12.3.2 Fixed-term sentences

- Where sentences are imposed for a definite period.

- CJA 2003: in sentences for more than 12 months, half of the period must be served.

- An offender remains on licence for the full term and can be returned to prison if conditions are breached.

12.3.3 Custody Plus

- s 181 CJA 2003: After three months in custody a period is spent undertaking a community sentence.

- The whole period cannot be more than 12 months.

- Requirements such as unpaid work, supervision, curfew or programme attendance can be attached.

12.3.4 Suspended sentences

- Time is only spent in custody (between 28–51 weeks) if the offender breaches terms of the supervision (which can be between six months and two years).

- This can be combined with a community order.

12.4 Community Orders

Under s 177 CJA 2003, courts can impose customised community sentences on those aged 16 or over combining one or more of the following requirements to meet the offender's needs:

Unpaid work	Activity	Curfew
• Between 40–300 hours	• Set activities carried out, e.g. contact with victim • Can apply to up to 60 separate days	• Can be ordered to remain at a fixed address • Can cover 2–12 hours in a 24-hour period • Can be enforced by electronic tagging
Exclusion	Supervision	Attendance centre
• s 205 CJA 2003 • A ban from entering specified place(s) • Can be complete or on certain days • Can last for up to two years	• Lasts from six months up to two years • Attendance is required at set appointments	• For under 25s

Other available requirements

- Residence

- Mental health treatment

- Drug rehabilitation

- Alcohol treatment

- Programme

- Prohibited activity

Research Point

Find five news stories which relate to crime and sentencing. Evaluate the balance which policymakers need to find between achieving justice for the victim and addressing the needs of the offender. Do you think that, in general, society supports the types of community orders outlined above?

12.5 Young Offenders

12.5.1 Custodial sentences

- The last resort.

- Young offenders are not housed alongside adults.

- There is a strong emphasis on education and training.

Sentences include:

Detention at Her Majesty's Pleasure
• Applied to an offender aged between 10 and 17 convicted of murder.
• A minimum sentence is recommended in keeping with the Sentencing Guidelines.
• The sentence initially is served in a special unit and then (after 21) in an adult prison.

Detention for serious crimes – additional sentencing powers
• s 53 Children and Young Persons Act 1933 – courts have the power in the case of serious offences to state that the young offender be detained for longer periods.
• For 10–13 year olds, the sentence must carry a maximum sentence of at least 14 years for adult offenders or be an offence of indecent assault on a woman.
• This power is also available for 14–17 year olds in relation to certain driving offences resulting in death.

Young Offenders' Institutions
• s 91 Powers of the Court (Sentencing) Act 2000: available for those aged from 18–20.
• Minimum sentence is 21 days.
• At the age of 21 the offender will be transferred to an adult prison.

Detention and training orders
• s 100 Powers of the Court (Sentencing) Act 2000: relates to an offender between 10–21.
• Sentence between 4–24 months, maximum six months for a summary offence.
• Offenders under 15: only made in relation to persistent offenders.
• Offenders under 12: only made if a custodial sentence is necessary to protect the public.

12.5.2 Youth Rehabilitation Orders

The following requirements can be attached to such an order:

- Activity
- Supervision
- Unpaid work (offenders between 16–17 at conviction)
- Programme
- Attendance centre
- Prohibited activity
- Curfew
- Exclusion
- Residence
- Local authority residence
- Mental health treatment
- Drug treatment
- Drug testing
- Intoxicating substance treatment
- Education
- Electronic monitoring.

12.6 Fines and Discharges

12.6.1 Fines

- Very commonly used in the Magistrates' Court, rarely in the Crown Court.
- Non-payment of fines leading to ineffective punishment and even imprisonment is a problem.

12.6.2 Discharges

12.6.2.1 Conditional

- Most commonly used particularly in Magistrates' Courts for first-time offenders who have committed a minor crime.
- States that the offender is discharged on condition of no further offences in a set period of time.

- If re-offending occurs, then the court can (on top of the penalty for the new offence) impose another sentence.

12.6.2.2 Absolute

- No penalty is imposed.

- Used where the offender is technically guilty but deemed not morally guilty.

12.7 Sentencing Practice

- A key aim of the Criminal Justice Act 2003 is to **reduce inconsistency in sentencing**.

- The Sentencing Council of England and Wales publishes sentencing guidelines.

- It therefore sets down various points the courts should follow.

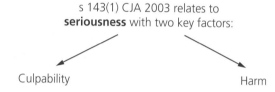

s 143(1) CJA 2003 relates to
seriousness with two key factors:

Culpability   Harm

Other aggravating factors of the CJA 2003, include:

- s 143(2): previous convictions.

- ss 145 and 146: if the offence was committed due to the victim's:

  - Race

  - Religion

  - Disability

  - Sexual orientation.

- High level of profit, attempt to conceal evidence, an abuse of trust, deliberate harm, targeting of the vulnerable are also taken into account.

Mitigating factors include:

- Provocation

- Mental illness or disability

- Youth or age which affects responsibility

- That the offender played a minor role in the offence.

Sentence reduction for a guilty plea

- s 144 CJA 2003
- Sentencing Guidelines state that a very early guilty plea should receive a reduction of up to one third unless prosecution case is overwhelming.
- This continues on a sliding scale with a one-tenth reduction if the trial has begun.

Thresholds

- s 152(2) CJA 2003: A custodial sentence should not be imposed unless justified.
- s 148(1) CJA 2003: A community sentence should not be imposed unless justified.

Pre-sentence reports

- Submitted by probation officer or social worker giving information about the offender's background and suitability for the range of community orders.
- Can be taken into account on assessing applying the threshold.
- s 156 CJA 2003: the report must be taken into account on applying a custodial or community sentence unless deemed not necessary.
- The report **must** be considered if the offender is under 18.
- If the defendant is mentally disordered then a medical report is required.

Workpoint

Explain to a visitor from another country the steps a court will take in choosing whether or not to impose a sentence and, if a sentence is imposed, the factors and issues they will take into account in determining this sentence.

12.8 Prison Statistics

In England and Wales:

- In 1951: 50 per 100,000 of the population were in prison.
- In 2010: 150 per 100,000 of the population were in prison.

This continues to be the highest rate in Europe.

59% of all prisoners will reoffend:

In December 2010, 84,548 people were remanded in custody:

- 5% of the prison population is female.

- 10,369 young adults (18–20 years old) are in custody.

- 1,572 juveniles (15–17 years old) are in custody.

- 273 12–15 year olds are in private secure training centres and 157 are in local authority secure children homes.

- 20% of British nationals in custody are from a minority ethnic group.

Workpoint

If the re-offending rate after custodial sentences is so high, to what extent do you believe that there is an argument for only using imprisonment for a very small number of serious crimes such as murder, manslaughter and rape?

Checkpoint

Task	Done
I can explain the different sentences available and key rules relating to their imposition	
I can outline the aims of punishment in the criminal justice system	
I know how the aims of punishment apply to young offenders	
I can analyse the nature of the aims of punishment and give examples of sentences which demonstrate each approach	
I can outline the different custodial sentences and when they will be imposed	
I know the requirements which can be attached to community orders	
I know key issues in relation to how sentences are imposed on young offenders	
I can outline the circumstances in which fines and discharges are ordered	
I understand general guidance in relation to sentencing practice	
I know the stages the court will follow to determine whether a sentence should be imposed and to determine the nature of any sentence	
I can outline key statistics in relation to the prison population of England and Wales	

Potential exam questions

1) Describe the main key aims of sentencing and evaluate their advantages and disadvantages.
2) Describe the different types of custodial and community sentences available.
3) How does the criminal justice system approach the sentencing of young offenders?
4) Describe the approach taken to sentencing laid down in the Criminal Justice Act 2003.

Glossary

Advance Indication of Sentence: Where the defendant instructs counsel to seek an indication from the judge of the maximum sentence which could be imposed if a guilty plea is entered. This is allowed in English law and follows the procedure laid down in *Goodyear* (2005) EWCA Crim 888.

- A 'basis of plea' document is submitted. This sets out the facts on which a guilty plea would be entered.

- The judge may either refuse to give an indication or give an indication which remains binding unless, after time for reasonable consideration, the defendant does not plead guilty.

This procedure is **not** followed in the Magistrates' Court.

After-the-event insurance: Insurance which allows claimants to insure against the risk of paying costs after a claim has begun. The premium has to be paid **before** the case begins. After s 29 Access to Justice Act 1999 the premium can now be claimed as part of court costs.

Alternative Business Structures: A business structure, provision for which is contained in the Legal Services Act 2007, in which legal professionals form partnerships with non-lawyers such as accountants, tax consultants and estate agents.

Appellate court: The court in which appeals are heard.

Cab-rank rule: Under paragraph 2 of the Code of Conduct of the Bar of England and Wales, a barrister must accept the brief which they are assigned and cannot refuse to provide services (this does not apply to the Public Access scheme).

'Call to the Bar': The procedure (by the four Inns of Court) by which students become barristers.

Conditional Fee Agreements: An agreement made by the lawyer and client that a success fee will be paid to the lawyer if the case is won. The lawyer does **not** gain a share of any damages awarded.

Criminal procedure rules: A set of rules, mainly codified in 2005 after the Auld Review, which relate to the practices and procedures in the criminal courts.

Default judgment: When judgment is given in favour of the claimant as the defendant has not filed the required documents in time.

Directed acquittal: When the judge at the end of the prosecution case directs the jury to acquit as he or she decides that in law the prosecution's evidence has not made out a case against the defendant. This happens in about 10% of cases.

Distinguishing: The process by which a past binding precedent is avoided by proving that its material facts were sufficiently different.

Domestic tribunals: 'In-house' tribunals set up by private bodies, e.g. to regulate professions or organisations such as universities. They must follow the rules of natural justice and are open to judicial review.

Ejusdem generis: 'Of the same kind'. General words are to be interpreted as being of the same kind as specific ones which come before them. There needs to be more than one specific word. We interpret the general terms according to the 'common and dominant' characteristics of the specific words.

Expressio unius est exclusio alterius: The mention of one thing excludes others. Where there is a closed set of words, then the statute **only** applies to those words and no others.

Golden rule: This builds upon the literal rule. The words of the statute are given their plain, ordinary meaning but if this results in an absurdity, then the statute can be interpreted to avoid this absurdity. This approach can be **narrow** – where a word has more than one meaning, choose the one which avoids the absurdity.

Hansard: An official word-for-word record of what is said in the proceedings and debates in Parliament.

ILEX: The Institute of Legal Executives, the awarding body for fully qualified legal executives. Fellowship of the Institute is a free-standing legal qualification. It has **22,000** members.

In force: Able to be relied upon in a court.

Judicial Studies Board (JSB): The organisation, established in 1978, which provides judicial training and advises on the training of lay magistrates and tribunal personnel. It:

- Organises refresher sessions
- Highlights areas of change or current interest
- Publishes books and guidance.

Lay people: People who are not legally qualified.

Leapfrog appeal: A civil appeal from the High Court can bypass the Court of Appeal and go straight to the Supreme Court. This can happen if the trial judge finds:

- A point of law of general public importance is involved.
- The point of law is one in which the judge is bound following the doctrine of stare decisis.
- The Supreme Court gives leave (permission) to appeal.

Literal rule: Give the words their plain, ordinary meaning even if this leads to a result which does not seem to make sense.

Material facts: The facts which are significant to the legal issue being decided in a case (they are the facts which matter!).

Mischief Rule: This is also known as the rule in *Heydon's Case* (1584). Following this approach, the judge will:

1. Determine what the common law was before the Act was passed.
2. Identify a mischief (e.g. what was wrong with the common law that Parliament sought to remedy with the passing of the Act).
3. Assume that Parliament created the Act to address this mischief and interpret the statute in the light of this.

Mock jury: A jury which watches or listens to a simulated case and then deliberates in front of cameras.

Noscitur a sociis: A word is known by the company it keeps.

Obiter dicta (plural)/*obiter dictum* (singular): 'Statements said by the way'/ 'A statement said by the way'. A statement or statements said in a case which do not form part of the *ratio decidendi* but can be **persuasive** (not binding!) in other cases.

Office for Judicial Complaints: An organisation established under the CRA 2005 with the power to investigate complaints about judges. These complaints, however, need to be upheld by the Lord Chancellor and Lord Chief Justice.

Paralegal: A general term to describe personnel who work in the legal field. They may or may not have formal legal qualifications. ILEX offers a recognised paralegal qualification. Paralegals may or may not attend court and may or may not be fee earners.

Per incuriam: 'Through lack of care'. If the judgment overlooked either a binding precedent or relevant statutory provision and, due to this, the final decision was incorrect.

Plea bargaining: Where the defendant pleads guilty in exchange for a reduction in sentence or pleads guilty to a lesser offence on the same facts. This is **not** accepted in English law. It benefits the prosecuting agencies but may:

• Create a feel of injustice for the victim/victim's family

• Lead to over-charging

• Put pressure on the defendant to accept a bargain.

Pro-bono work: 'for the public good'. Advice for those who cannot afford to pay, given, for example by the Free Representation Unit (FRU). Many law schools have successful, supported *pro-bono* schemes.

Professional indemnity insurance: The insurance that all solicitors in private practice need to hold in case of a finding of negligent loss to a client.

Purposive approach: Interpret the law in the light of its wider general aims and principles. This particularly applies when interpreting a statute in the light of EU law. However, this approach is becoming increasingly more common throughout the English legal system.

Ratio decidendi: 'The reason for deciding'. The legal principle upon which a case is decided in the light of the material facts (it is the part of the case which is binding).

Reverse: Where a higher court reaches a different decision from a lower court as the same case travels up the court hierarchy.

Royal Assent: No Bill can become an Act without the Royal Assent. Traditionally this means that the monarch must consent to the Bill becoming law. However, this is merely a formal process: the monarch does not read every Bill and give personal consent (it has not been withheld since 1707).

Shadow jury: A jury which sits in a courtroom and withdraws at the same time as the actual jury but its deliberations take place in front of cameras. *The Shadow Jury at Work* (1974) found that shadow juries take their work very seriously.

Stare decisis: 'Stand by cases already decided'. When a legal principle has been decided in one case then this *has* to be followed in certain other courts.

Summary judgment: Where the defendant has filed the correct documents within the given time but the defence masks the true defence. The court has the power in these circumstances to find for the claimant.

Trial courts/courts of first instance: The court in which the case is heard for the first time.

Index